Case Studies in
Asian
Management

Editor

Parissa HAGHIRIAN
Sophia University, Japan

 **World Scientific**

NEW JERSEY · LONDON · SINGAPORE · BEIJING · SHANGHAI · HONG KONG · TAIPEI · CHENNAI

Published by

World Scientific Publishing Co. Pte. Ltd.

5 Toh Tuck Link, Singapore 596224

USA office: 27 Warren Street, Suite 401-402, Hackensack, NJ 07601

UK office: 57 Shelton Street, Covent Garden, London WC2H 9HE

Library of Congress Cataloging-in-Publication Data
Case studies in Asian management / edited by Parissa Haghirian (Sophia University, Japan).
  pages cm
  ISBN 978-9814508971 (hardcover : alk. paper)
  1. Management--Asia--Case studies. I. Haghirian, Parissa, 1970–
HD70.A7C37 2013
658.0095--dc23
                                    2013009942

British Library Cataloguing-in-Publication Data
A catalogue record for this book is available from the British Library.

In-house Editor: Monica Lesmana

Typeset by Stallion Press
Email: enquiries@stallionpress.com

Printed in Singapore

Contents

About the Authors

Thomas Anderson III received his BS in Economics from St. John's University in Minnesota, USA and his Masters in International Business and Development from Sophia University's Graduate Program of Global Studies in Tokyo. He currently works as a tax associate for PricewaterhouseCoopers in Tokyo.

John Paul Datugan Antes is a career civil servant in the Philippine government. He has served the Philippine Senate and the Philippine Council for the Welfare of Children. He is presently connected with the Philippine Sugar Regulatory Administration. He earned his Master's degree in Public Administration from the University of the Philippines-Diliman in 2008 and his Master of Arts in International Business and Development Studies from Sophia University, Tokyo, Japan in 2011 through Japan Development Scholarship (JDS). He plans to pursue his Ph.D in the near future.

Parissa Haghirian is Associate Professor of International Management at the Faculty of Liberal Arts at Sophia University in Tokyo, Japan. She is a visiting professor at Groupe HEC in Paris, Aalto University, Keio Business School, and an adjunct professor at Temple University in Tokyo. Parissa holds a master's degree in Japanese Studies (University of Vienna) and a master's and doctorate degrees in International Management (Vienna University of Business,

Austria). She has published several books and articles on the topic and is the author of *Understanding Japanese Management Practices.*

Marc David Hercaud graduated in 2012 from the ESSCA School of Management, France, holding a Master's degree in Banking and Risk Management. He did in 2010/11 a one-semester exchange program at Sophia University's Graduate Program in Global Studies, Tokyo. He is now working as a Treasury & Corporate Finance Officer for RTL Group (leading European mass media network), Luxembourg.

Emi Inamoto graduated in 2010 from the Faculty of Liberal Arts at Sophia University, Tokyo, Japan, with a major in International Business and Economics. Upon graduation, she attended Waseda University for one-year to focus on the Japanese Language. She now works as an assistant buyer for Storage plants, mainly, Liquified Natural Gas (LNG) plants at Japan's leading heavy industries company.

Mai Kaneshiro graduated in March 2012 from the Faculty of Liberal Arts in Sophia University, where she majored in International Business and Economics. After graduation, she has been working at Google inc. Japan office.

TingHsuan Kuo received her BS in Economics from National Taiwan University and did a one-year exchange program at Hokkaido University in Japan. She is currently pursuing her Masters in International Business and Development at Sophia University's Graduate Program of Global Studies. Her research primarily focused on Japan–Taiwan business alliance in the Chinese market.

Christian Knuth graduated as Industrial Engineer majoring in Chemical Process Engineering at the Berlin Institute of Technology. He studied abroad at Sophia University from 2010 until 2011 in Tokyo with a focus on International Business and Development issues e.g., resource economics and environment. He finished his diploma thesis on process costs of carbon dioxide capture and storage technologies at Volkswagen Group's R&D department in 2012.

Kaoutar Lazrak received her Master's degree in Marketing in Rouen Business School, France. She was an exchange student at the Sophia University's Graduate Program in Global Studies in Tokyo, Japan. Kaoutar worked as a Sales & Marketing intern in luxury hotels like Aldrovandi Villa Borghese, Rome and La Mamounia Marrakech, Morocco.

Dr. Anselmo B. Mercado is a retired Professor of Rural-Social Development in the College of Agriculture, Xavier University, Cagayan de Oro City, Philippines. He was Director of the South East Asia Rural Social Leadership Institute (SEARSOLIN), Xavier University (1993–2007), former Dean of the College of Agriculture, Xavier University (1998–2000). He holds a Bachelor's Degree in Agriculture, major in Animal Husbandry, from Xavier University (1963), a Master's Degree in Adult Education from the Virginia Polytechnic Institute and State University, USA (1973), and a Doctorate Degree in Education from North Carolina State University, USA (1985). He has chaired the Study Committee and the Steering Committee in the crusade for making the Water District a cooperative (since December 2007 up to the present.) He was elected as chairman of the interim Board of Directors of the WATERCCOOP.

Beatrice Reboux grew up in Charente Maritime, South West France. She graduated from ESLSCA American business school in Paris with degrees in Management and Entrepreneurship. She moved to Japan in 2010 and entered Sophia University in 2011. There, she studied International Business and Development Studies while working part-time for a japanese consulting company. Beatrice Reboux is interested in cross cultural behavior, mainly Japanese corporate behavior. She practices yoga and loves traveling.

David Trappolini graduated in 2013 from Louvain School of Management in Belgium with a Master's degree in Business Engineering. From 2012 to 2013, he attended in an exchange program at Sophia University in Tokyo where he participated in the Graduate program in Global Studies. During his internship in an energy company in Brussels, he completed a Master's thesis on the application of activity-based costing concepts to transmission tariffs of electricity.

Tu Jiawen received her Bachelor's degree in Law from Wuhan University, China and a Master's degree from Sophia University in Japan majoring in International Business and Development.

Xiaozhou Wu is currently a consultant in the Transaction Advisory Services Ernst & Young in Germany. He holds a Master of Science degree in business administration at Ludwig-Maximilian-University of Munich, Germany. He received his bachelor's degree in business administration from Zhejiang University, China in 2010.

Introduction

ASIAN CORPORATIONS ARE BECOMING INCREASINGLY IMPORTANT IN INTERNATIONAL MANAGEMENT

In the last decades many Asian corporations have gone through an impressive growth and development process, changing from classic manufacturing firms with a focus on production styles and cost effectiveness into innovation- and change-oriented multinational corporations developing fashionable and successful products for consumers all over the world.

This change has not gone unnoticed in Western industrialized countries. Asian corporations have become more dominant in economic news. They have become a major point of discussion in business classrooms as well, where students show increasing interest in corporations and management styles of Asian corporations.

Even if there is a great interest on how Asian corporations act and how they are being managed, a few topics dominate the discussion in the West. Two main issues featured in the news are technology and copyright infringements. Labor conditions are disscussed, as are challenges of Western firms entering Asian markets.

As important as these topics are from a legal and human rights perspective, there is little information on Asian management styles and corporate strategies. Asian management styles are often portrayed as exotic and very particular. They differ from Western management styles, but the differences are only visible if Asian companies do not comply with Western ideas of business or if they are more successful than Western corporations. Furthermore, information on Asian management is often distorted and communicated with many stereotypes.

However, we also need to look at management practices and strategies in greater detail. Not only can we learn a very new and inspiring view of management we also need to investigate how Asian markets and their enterprises develop.

Many Asian managers have Western business degrees or long experience dealing with Western business partners. As we know our management practices better than we know theirs, this leaves Asian managers with more possible choices. For each management problem, they can find not only an Asian solution but also look for inspiration and answers among Western management styles.

With the rising importance of Asian companies as competitors and business partners, we therefore need to learn more about them. This development can be found in the Western media but not always perceived very objectively. The rapid development of multinational corporations in Asia still leaves us with a lot of questions. How are Asian companies managed and which philosophies do they follow? Are Asian management practices truly different from "traditional" Western management practices? What differences can we observe between different Asian nations and their corporations? And finally: How do Asian corporations cooperate, communicate and work within Asia?

INTENTION OF THIS BOOK

It is obvious that there is a lack of knowledge on how corporations in Asia develop strategies, organize their work processes and deal with competition. Western managers and business students need to know more about Asian corporations and management styles. Learning about Asia, however, has always been a challenging task. The main challenge is the complexity we encounter when dealing with Asian management issues. We are not talking only of very many different countries, but also different types of businesses, not to mention national management preferences and styles.

This book tries to fill this gap, by presenting case studies of various Asian countries. This book will not be able to reduce the complexity of the topics. The presented case studies are as diverse as management activities in Asia and include a variety of different companies in several Asian countries.

I try to focus on intra-Asian activities to show that many challenges that companies here face are very similar to the ones Western corporation meet when entering Asian markets. I would also like to show that even if challenges are similar, solutions are often very different. All cases provide background material on the companies described and also give an overview on their historical background.

CONTENTS OF THIS BOOK

The book consists of six sections. Six nations and their companies operating in each nation are described. The first country is the People's Republic of China. The first case in Section I described a Japanese corporation and its challenges entering the promising Chinese market. In her case "FamilyMart's China Expansion" TsingHsuan Kuo describes the challenges of a market entry in China. She shows that it is not only European and American firms which have to deal with cultural, logistical and operative problems when doing business in China, but also China's neighbor Japan. FamilyMart is busy developing Asian strategies so as to achieve its goals in the world's most popular market. The company developed very ambitious market entry goals, but has to overcome a number of market entry barriers. Answers to questions have to be found: Is China the right market for FamilyMart to realize its growth goal? What can FamilyMart do to overcome the obstacles it faces in the Chinese market, and how can FamilyMart enhance its overall competency to facilitate its expansion plans in China?

The second case in Section I "Ali Baba: Facing its Thieves" by Xiaozhou Wu discusses an important topic: unethical business. In this case however, we do not find an Asian company ignoring Western standards, but a Chinese company dealing with customers and their unethical behaviors. The case describes the rise and success of alibaba.com, one of China's most famous Internet businesses. Company founder Jack Ma created an influential company conglomerate by offering an online market place for businesses interested in the Chinese market. However, as the company grows, trouble too grows. Some of alibaba.com's customers used the homepage to commit fraud and cheat other members. The company faces a decrease in customer trust and needs to change it strategy.

Case three in the first section covers a Chinese corporation which has grown into a serious competitor in the global sportswear industry: Li Ning. The case written by Tu Jiawen describes how Li Ning became one of China's best known sports brands. Founded by a well-known Chinese athlete Mr. Li Ning, the company rose from a small sports good producer to become the sponsor and sportswear provider of the Chinese National Team at the Olympic Games. The company also made news in the West, when it launched a new slogan and logo which strongly resembled that of their competitors Nike.

The interaction of politics and business is often discussed in business media. These interactions also interfere with customer relations and profits. Asian corporations trying to do business are no exepction here. The case about Shiseido by Kaoutar Lazrak describes how the Japanese cosmetic giant successfully entered the Chinese market, which quickly became its most important overseas market. But politics interfered with the ongoing successes. As the Japanese and Chinese governments got into a dispute about the Senkaku Islands, Chinese consumers started to boycott Japanese products. The company has to develop strategies to deal with anti-Japanese feelings to sustain their profits in the Chinese market.

The second nation that has influenced Asian management processes is Japan. Japan has become a very interesting business place when learning about Asian management practices. Not only does Japan have fully developed — and in many areas — saturated market, Japanese consumers are highly sophisticated and give us an idea as to which directions consumers in other Asian markets may develop.

Japan is the only post-industrialized country in Asia and during the past 60 years not only witnessed an incredible economic boom, but also developed into the richest country in Asia. Japanese companies maintain very close links with the special Japanese management style, which is characterized by features such as lifetime employment, extraordinary corporate loyalty and high employee motivation. Also famous are Japanese production techniques which have gained recognition throughout the world.

The first case I present here is one of the most successful Japanese enterprises: Uniqlo. Uniqlo applied a very special mix of traditional Japanese and Western-profit management practices and has grown from a small business into one of the major global players in the apparel industry. Tadashi Yanai, the owner of the company became the richest man in Japan. And although the apparel industry is not a particularly highly innovative industry, the case study shows how the company was able to use traditional Japanese manufacturing techniques to save costs and improve quality but at the same time push innovation and growth with very particular and uncommon strategies. In the case study, the rise of the company and its current situation is described. However, even the most successful company has rivals. Uniqlo's sales in Japan are threatened by aggressive competitors and the company needs to develop new ideas to sustain its competitive advantage.

The second Japanese case study looks at Japanese marketing. In his case "The Suntory Highball Revolution: Can a Type of Drink Save an Industry?" Thomas Andersen III describes how the Japanese Whiskey producer Suntory has revived its image and sales by using very special marketing strategies. The challenge for Suntory has been to make an old product seem new as well as appeal to a wide range of consumers. After trying several times to revive the market without any success, Suntory seemed to be out of options. The company started to see success when they re-introduced a popular drink during the bubble economy, the whisky highball cocktail. Suntory has reworked its strategies and with the help of their "new" drink — the whiskey highball — the Japanese market has been more aware of whiskey. But the Japanese market is known for booms and fads, Japanese consumers pick up trends quickly only to move on to the next trend. The question Suntory faces is whether this Highball Boom can be sustained.

Japanese electronic manufacturers have for many decades dominated the worldwide industry. They were famous for their cost effective and quality approach. However in the past years they also made news, because of the slow and often ineffective reactions to an increasing global and competitive business environment. Many of the former industry giants face serious difficulties at the moment. Often, traditional Japanese management styles and and the Japanese aversion to risk are blamed for these problems. But not all of Japanese electric corporations are the same. David Trappolini shows in his case "A Tale of Three Companies — Survival Strategies of Sony, Hitachi and Canon" how three different Japanese firms Sony, Canon and Hitachi rose in the last century, the challenges they faced — and still face — and how they have developed very different strategies to deal with the current economic situation.

India is another major player in Asian management. The country has proven to be a successful manufacturer of goods, not only for Western firm, but also Asian ones. In the case "Doing It the Toyota Way in India? Managing Unsettled Labor Relations at Toyota Kirloskar" Christian Knuth describes on how cross-cultural differences and misunderstandings can also be observed within Asian cooperations. Japanese automaker Toyota for example faced very tough times when setting up a production site in India. No less than four strikes and two factory lock-outs (one lasting for 53 days) led to serious confrontations between the management and the employees, who were represented by their labor union. Since the two largest cases of labor unrest were banned by the state government rather than being successfully solved within the company, trusting cooperation between management and workers is not likely to develop in the short term. The case shows that labor issues are often undermined by cultural differences — a challenge that does not only concern Western corporations entering Asian markets to reduce factor costs.

Another booming business nation is Korea. Korean companies such as Samsung and Hyundai have lately dominated the news by offering innovative- and customer-oriented consumer goods without fear of global competition. However, the road to success is still under construction for some Korean firms. The case study "KIA Motors facing Globalization Challenges" written by Marc David Hercaud describes the attempts of Korean car maker KIA to become a global player. From roots as a typical Korean conglomerate, the company has achieved vast domestic reach as well as global success, with the KIA brand now the second biggest seller in South Korea and the group the fifth biggest seller worldwide. KIA is currently facing a particular challenge in Western countries, especially in Europe: changing and improving brand image and brand identity — a challenging task.

The final nation featured in this book is often neglected when discussing Asian Business: The Philippines. An aspiring business nation, the Philippines has to face a number of challenges in its economic development. The two cases show that corruption and the different levels of economic development across the country play a major role in slowing down growth.

In this case "Brightening Philippine Airliness (PAL): Strategizing for the Future of Asia's Pioneer and Sunniest Air Transporter" John Paul D. Antes describes the rise of the Philippines first airline. The company has a long history that started early after the war. After privatization, the company started to become a professional business that expands globally. But the corporation also faces increasing challenges. Not only are there labor relations problems to deal with, it also faces competition from the Philippines rising budget airline — Cebu Pacific. How they will succeed in an increasingly competitive environment remains to be seen.

The second case in Section IV shows another facet of Philippino Business, a consumers cooperative in one of the thousands of Philippine islands attempting to improve the living conditions of the local population. The case called "The Birth of the Water Consumers Cooperative" by Anselmo B. Mercado describes the struggles of setting up a Water Cooperative in Cagayan de Oro City, Northern Mindanao, Philippines. It discusses the major events and activities of the crusade that led to the birth of the cooperative, its future prospects and challenges in its quest to own, operate and manage the Water District, which if realized, would be the first of its kind in the Philippines. The case also presents the cooperative's idea, its main purposes and advantages as an alternative to other forms of enterprises in the operation of the Water District.

The final section of the book deals with cross-cultural encounters of Asians. Here personal intercultural encounters are described and discussed. Both authors are Asian and describe their international experiences and how they deal with them. Here Mai Kaneshiro describes how she visited her Australian friend's home and family for the first time and was surprised how differently visitors were treated. However, she could quickly recognize that these differences were not only culturally very different, but that hospitality could take very different forms.

The second mini case in this section describes a Korean student's experiences in Japan. Entering an international university in Japan, she met students from other cultures. Her first encounter remained memorable, a few Western girls hugged and kissed her on the cheek when saying hello. Her first reaction was shock as she was not used to this kind of intimacy. When she put her arms around her friend's arm, she was met with a similar reaction. She learned that being close to someone means something very different across cultures.

I would like to thank Ben Young of Babel Editing and Franziska Ferdinand for their support in editing this book.

This book attempts to present an overview on the variety and complexity of management and business processes in Asian countries. It intends to support business people and students of international management to get a deeper understanding of Asian management practices, by presenting practical examples of Asian firms and their strategies.

Parissa Haghirian
Sophia University
June 2013

Section I

THE PEOPLE'S REPUBLIC OF CHINA

FamilyMart's China Expansion

TsingHsuan Kuo

> *"We are transforming FamilyMart from a Japanese into a global brand—*
> *for faster growth, on a bigger stage."*
> Shiro Inoue, Managing Director (2010)

The first convenience store (CVS) that opened in Japan was Seven-Eleven in 1974. The convenience store concept innovated grocery shopping in Japan. The self-service sales system of the supermarket that offers a wide variety of food and household merchandise with a low price had been broadly received by the consumers.

Despite being an American retail concept, Japanese consumers embraced the idea of shopping for groceries 24/7 and CVS became a common site in Japanese cities. The CVS concept had been dramatically refined by Japanese's know-how on CVS chain operations allowing customers not only to buy products, but also to pay bills, buy baseball tickets, fax, print, copy and send parcels. Even during the depression and low consumption rates after the bursting of the bubble, the convenience store industry had grown rapidly and developed tremendously, becoming "the life infrastructure" in Japan. A new retail shop type, the Japanese convenience story conquered Japan.[1] The new shopping concept became very popular and the traditional retail stores were left behind.

---

[1] FamilyMart Homepage, http://www.family.co.jp/english/investor_relations/management_strategy/index.html. [20 November 2011]

11

During the depression and low consumption rates after the bursting of the bubble, the CVS had grown rapidly and developed tremendously, becoming "the life infrastructure" in Japan. The CVS industry was dramatically refined by the Japanese and their know-how on CVS chain operations. According to the Japan Franchise Association, the number of the convenience stores in Japan had reached 43,291 by the end of 2010.[2] Among them, the three largest chains are Seven-Eleven, Lawson and FamilyMart.

The CVS industry relies heavily on the point of sales in which food is the main product. Since the unit price of its products is low, the CVS chain makes low margins. As their stores sizes are limited, there is not much room for stock, and thus products have to be delivered multiple times per day. As a result, a well-constructed distribution system is important for running a convenience store chain. In many cases, several stores from the same chain operate in neighboring areas in order to make distribution to each store cheaper. It also makes multiple distributions per day possible.

Recently, the CVS industry in Japan has been approaching saturation and the Japanese CVS chains have found themselves under increasing pressure to grow their business in the domestic market. To strengthen its competence, the Japanese CVS chains expanded their businesses overseas in other Asian nations since the 1980s. With their know-hows, the Japanese CVS chains succeeded in growing their businesses and became the main market players in these regions. For example in Taiwan, Seven-Eleven and FamilyMart are the two largest CVS chains, while in Korea, FamilyMart and Lawson are the main players.[3]

Since the year 2000, however Japanese CVS chains have found themselves under increasing pressure over the past few years due to the market saturation and aging problems. Overseas expansion seemed a good solution for FamilyMart, one of the main players in

---

[2] Convenience Store FC Statistic (from January 2010 to December 2010) Japan Franchise Association, http://www.jfa-fc.or.jp/misc/static/pdf/cvs_2010_11.pdf. [6 January 2011]

[3] Convenience Store to fight market saturation (http://business.nikkeibp.co.jp/article/manage/20101018/216707/?P=2). [October 2010]

the Japanese CVS market. In order to help increase its competitive competence in the challenging domestic market, FamilyMart has been expanding to other Asian nations since 1980. Twenty years after the overseas expansion began with the entry into the Taiwanese market in 1988, the number of the oversea stores (8,948 stores as the end of 2010) had exceeded the domestic ones. FamilyMart has the largest number of stores overseas in comparison to its Japenese competitors.[4]

While the businesses in Taiwan and Korea have grown successfully, the Chinese market, which is regarded as the main driver of the future growth, proved to be more difficult. The company not only has expansion hurdles brought on by local infrastructure and Chinese business practices, it also faces competition from other local and foreign chains. The goal under the Pan-Pacific plan that 'aimed to build a global network of 20,000 stores by fiscal Year 2008[5]' had failed with only a store number of 14,651 as of February 2009.[6] FamilyMart had to modify its plan and aim to reach a total of 25,000 stores worldwide by fiscal year 2015.[7]

FAMILYMART PROFILE

The first FamilyMart store opened in Saitama, Japan. It was a test store under the Seiyu Group's plan to operate a mini-store chain. The name "FamilyMart" represents the company's philosophy of hospitality. In addition, it also means that "the entire chain is a strong bond akin to family ties, in which both the head office and the partners strive together to achieve mutual prosperity and growth". Under the slogan "FamilyMart, Where You Are One of the Family", FamilyMart

---

[4] FamilyMart Annual Report 2010 (http://www.family.co.jp/english/investor_relations/annual_report/2010.html). [30 October 2011]

[5] FamilyMart, 2005, *Expanding the Pan Pacific Branch of the Family Tree* (http://www.family.co.jp/english/investor_relations/annual_report/pdf/05_e_03.pdf). [30 October 2011]

[6] FamilyMart Annual Report 2009, http://www.family.co.jp/company/investor_relations/library/annual_report/pdf/09/j05.pdf. [1 December 2010]

[7] FamilyMart Annual Report 2010.

wants to ensure that the customers enjoy every moment they spend in a FamilyMart store through developing the "FamilyMart Feel".[8]

With the establishment of Family Co., Ltd. in 1981, FamilyMart became independent form the Seiyu Group. Being able to stand on its own feet, FamilyMart started to expand the network in Japan. Attitudes towards spending shifted during the economic fluctuations of Japan's bubble economy, FamilyMart increased its number of outlets and took an innovative approach toward its products and service offerings.

FamilyMart had been grown rapidly during the 1980s. Beginning with a store number of less than 100, FamilyMart became a CVS chain with more than 1,000 stores in 1987. The customer base was growing as well. In the same year, FamilyMart became a listed company and introduced the FamilyMart brand with a standardized FamilyMart design. Product development was included into FamilyMart's business, and various in-store services such as delivery, copying and photo printing was provided.

During the 1990s, FamilyMart further improved the store functions, and aimed to construct itself as a "life infrastructure". Through developing a new concept for CVS operations, FamilyMart wanted to provide its customers a feeling that "*conbini nanoni kokomadeyaruno*" (tr. Although it's (only) a CVS, you can do it all here).

In the 21st century, FamilyMart has grown into the third largest CVS chain in Japan behind Seven-Eleven and Lawson. To accelerate the growth pace, the company has been aggressively exploring the overseas market and aims to develop "FamilyMart" into a global brand.

One of FamilyMart's store functions in Japan is providing the "Osaifu Service". As the pioneer of e-money service in Japan's retail industry, FamilyMart further innovated the payment process by cooperating with NTT DoCoMo, Japan's leading telecommunications company. Thus, in 2007 FamilyMart formed a strategic alliance with NTT DoCoMo and began accepting mobile credit *via* DoCoMo's iD platforms enabling customers to complete the payment process simply by waving their phones over a reader/writer.

---

[8] FamilyMart Annual Report 2011 (http://www.family.co.jp/english/investor_relations/annual_report/pdf/11/e02f.pdf). [6 January 2011]

To build customer's loyalty, FamilyMart joined in the T-Point Loyalty Program in 2007, which is one of the largest joint-point programs in Japan, combining the previous Famima Cards with the new point-loyalty T-cards with a 34 million member base nationwide. In that way FamilyMart could not only improve its customer relations, but also increase its customer base.

After the acquisition of the 7th largest CVS am/pm chain in 2010, the market share of FamilyMart in Japan further increased. Despite the success in the domestic market, FamilyMart considers overseas expansions as the chain's main driver for growth. As the most aggressive chain in exploring the overseas market, FamilyMart expects itself to develop a "global standard" and a broader standpoint to continuously deal with all the challenges in the continually internationalizing global market.

FIRST GLOBAL OPERATIONS

Since the 1980s, FamilyMart began constructing its global network to shift its focus away from the saturated Japanese market. In 1988, in its first wave of overseas expansion, FamilyMart chose Taiwan as the first foreign market, and entered the Korean market in 1990 and Thailand in 1992. The chain overseas had been growing and the store number in these three regions exceeded 2,000 in 2001. With its successful operations in the overseas market, the overall number of FamilyMart stores reached 10,000, with 6,102 in Japan and 3,898 overseas, at the end of 2003.

At this point of time, FamilyMart started to focus on developing overseas markets for further expanding its business. Thus, the next stage of network expansion included setting up stores in regions FamilyMart has not yet entered, while increasing the number of stores where FamilyMart already has a presence.

The first FamilyMart store in China opened in Shanghai with the establishment of Shanghai FamilyMart Co., Ltd. The next year, FamilyMart entered the American market with a "Famima" store in Los Angeles. To accelerate the pace of expansion, Guangzhou FamilyMart and Suzhou FamilyMart were established in China in

Table 1.   The growth of FamilyMart Chains.

Number of stores

Legend: Japan, Taiwan, Korea, Thailand, China, U.S.A, VietNam, Indonesia

FYE 2/2009   FYE 2/2010   FYE 2/2011   FYE 2/2012   FYE 2/2013

Source: FamilyMart Homepage (http://www.family.co.jp/english/investor_relations/stores.html)

2006 and 2007 (See Table 1). As the latest step of its global expansion, FamilyMart set up a business in Vietnam in 2009.

With the goal of reaching a total of 25,000 stores worldwide by 2015, FamilyMart expanded its business simultaneously in Japan and overseas.

Taiwan was FamilyMart's first overseas market. Entering in year 1988, FamilyMart had reached a successful operation with 2,424 stores. Becoming a listed company, Taiwan FamilyMart Co., Ltd. was established as a public company in 2002 and has grown steadily into Taiwan's second largest CVS chain. Although the market competition has become tougher, FamilyMart increases its market share and competitiveness through providing innovative new ready-to-eat products and improving the store service, for example, by offering e-money services.

South Korea's market, where FamilyMart is operating the most stores, is considered to have more growth potential. Having entered the Korean market in 1990, FamilyMart has grown into the country's largest chain with a store number approaching 5,000. To further accelerate store openings in the increasingly strict CVS industry in Korea, FamilyMart differentiates itself from other competitors by providing high quality food and other ready-to-eat items and by introducing its own "FamilyMart" brand. The following strategies were developed for market entries outside Japan:

Strategy 1: Forming Joint Ventures as the basic movement overseas

FamilyMart's basic movement in developing business overseas is to form joint ventures with local companies.[9] In addition to sharing the risk in the new markets and enhancing the profitability, there are two main reasons for FamilyMart to choose this kind of entry mode. First, a successful retail business requires a localized business model. A company cannot simply copy the domestic one to the new markets without adjusting it. FamilyMart therefore provides the overseas chain with its own CVS operation concepts, systems and know-how, and then adjusts them based on the ideas and advices of its local partners who have abundant experience and knowledge of the local market.[10] Through this process, local requirements can be taken into account, while quality standards can be kept.

Another strategy was to build a strong relation with the joint venture partners in order to support the growth of the business in the new market. Although FamilyMart could enter the market easily by licensing the brand, thus facing less risk,[11] it instead aims to reinforce the FamilyMart business with the venture partners by cooperating and pooling each other's strengths. By combining their resources and focusing on those areas where they have an advantage, the performance and position of FamilyMart can be further strengthened.

---

[9] In 1990, FamilyMart entered the Korea market through a franchise contract with the local real estate agent Bokwang Group, transferring the CVS know-how and FamilyMart logo under license. So far, Korea is the only area that FamilyMart entered through licensing. In 1990 FamilyMart entered the Korean market under a license agreement with the Korean Bokwang Group. The foreign exchange law required domestically ownership, but FamilyMart Japan bought a 25% stake in 1999 when the law was relaxed.

[10] FamilyMart Homepage.

[11] *Ibid.*

These measures not only help to develop business in overseas markets, it might bring some changes for the Japanese head office as well. For example, Taiwan FamilyMart CEO Jin-Ting Pan was appointed as the top manager of Shanghai FamilyMart before he was selected as one of the managing executive officers of FamilyMart Japan.

Strategy 2: Becoming a "Global Group"

What is more important than directly participating in the business, is to construct a "FamilyMart Global Group". Each year, FamilyMart holds an "Area Franchisers' Summit" where all of the overseas corporate franchisers and the Japanese headquarter gather, to discuss and coordinate the company's policy. By converging and exchanging their opinions, both the Japanese headquarter and the overseas chains are better able to achieve mutual growth and success. Furthermore through this process, closer relationships can be built among all the group members, helping mutual trust and commitment to become FamilyMart's foundation and developing the company into a global brand.

Strategy 3: A close relation with the parent company

Another characteristic is the strong cooperation with Itochu, a related company.[12] In the FamilyMart–Itochu alliance, Itochu enters the overseas markets together with FamilyMart and has been providing its own resources to strengthen FamilyMart's overall competency. Itochu, which aimed to construct "an integrated system" of the value chain, has internalized FamilyMart's value chain and expanded its own business into related sectors producing commodities for FamilyMart, including food containers, textiles and the company's own truck.

---

[12] Itochu is one of the leading *sogo shosha* (trading firm) in Japan, with approximately 150 bases in 74 countries. The business of Itochu includes domestic trading, import/export, and overseas trading of various products such as textiles, machineries, information and communications technologies, aerospace, electronics, energy, metals, minerals, chemicals, forest products, general merchandise, food, finance, realty, insurance, and logistics services, as well as business investments in Japan and overseas.

In Taiwan, FamilyMart and Itochu invested together in a local food manufacturer to produce the ready-to-eat items. Also, through joint venture, Itochu established a distribution company to distribute the goods for FamilyMart. With the CVS operation and logistic know-how transferred between FamilyMart and Itochu, such as inventory control, product processing and sanitary management, the distribution system, service standards and CVS operations in Taiwan are considered very similar to the Japanese ones. Meanwhile, Itochu has also been constructing the distribution system in Korea since the establishment of Bokwang FamilyMart. In 2002, Itochu invested in a Korean food plant and provided it with the know-how on food processing. With the Japanese technology, the factory is currently supplying high quality and sanitary ready-to-eat items to Bokwang FamilyMart — what differentiated the company from its local competitors.

ASIAN CHALLENGES

Despite the successful achievements in the Taiwanese and Korean markets, FamilyMart faced several challenges while expanding the business.

Developing a CVS chain business in a foreign country takes time and money. Despite the successful achievements overseas, it took a long period for FamilyMart's business in Taiwan, Thailand and Korea to really start growing.[13] Table 2 suggests the low growing rate for stores in Taiwan in the beginning. For FamilyMart, one of the main methods to achieve market success is to differentiate itself from the local chains through bento (a popular Japanese lunch boxes) and other ready-to-eat products. Although possessing the know-how of product innovation and logistics, in some overseas areas the necessary facilities, logistic networks and other infrastructures used to produce these food items cannot be acquired. Thus, FamilyMart either had to build them by their own or have partners provide them.

---

[13] FamilyMart Annual Report 2010 (http://www.family.co.jp/english/investor_relations/annual_report/pdf/10/e04.pdf). [June 2012]

Table 2.   FamilyMart's store growth in Taiwan.

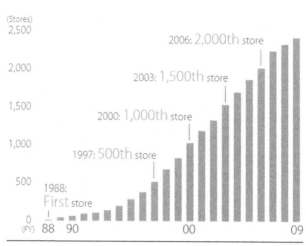

Source: FamilyMart Homepage (http://www.family.co.jp/eng-lish/investor_relations/annual_report/pdf/10/e04.pdf). [June 2012]

Besides, the advantage of logistics and product innovation only can become existent after a certain business scale is reached. After reaching that point, profits might increase alongside the rise of the store number. Thus, it takes time for a CVS business to break even. If the store number stagnates (there were only 10 FamilyMarts stores in the US, five years after market entry), a company has to have strong financial background and assistance, and choose the right markets for the chain to grow.[14]

Also, since the retail sector is an industry which requires high level of localization, FamilyMart could not simply copy the Japanese system to the overseas markets. The company had to adapt to the new environment and develop a system that fitted the host market. For example, the CVS industry in Japan is well developed and became a senior market. Many of the markets outside Japan however, were

---

[14] K. Chisachi, "*Shijō no hōwa to tatakau konbini ensustoa*" *Nikkei Business Online*, http://business.nikkeibp.co.jp/article/manage/201018/216707/p=2.

still in early developing stages. Thus, to expand successfully in a foreign market, FamilyMart had to create different models for different areas.[15]

When forming a joint venture, the ownership structure is usually considered as an important issue. FamilyMart however, considers commitment from each party and inter-partner trust-building more crucial. However, partner selection is not an easy process in the initial stage. As it took 10 years to achieve the first 500 stores in Taiwan, FamilyMart had learned the importance of selecting the right partner.[16] FamilyMart entered Taiwan with a joint venture with the Panvest Group. However in 1998, Panvest Group went into bankruptcy after the Asian Financial Crisis and put Taiwan FamilyMart into severe financial difficulties. Facing this unexpected event, FamilyMart had to deviate from its original plan of holding only a minority stake of Taiwan FamilyMart and made the decision of acquiring stock together with Itochu. Subsequently, they became the largest stockholders. Under FamilyMart's and Itochu's cooperation, Taiwan FamilyMart developed well and expanded rapidly into the country's second largest chain. By overcoming the difficulties together, the FamilyMart–Itochu Group and Taiwan FamilyMart developed mutual trust and a strong commitment toward the business. The FamilyMart–Itochu group also acquired various resources from the Taiwan FamilyMart which included the accumulated know-how of setting up businesses in a foreign country as well as experienced manpower being able to cooperate with the Japanese headquarter in its global business.[17]

---

[15] I. Kazuya and Y. Akira, 2009, "*Ion, Konbini de chūgoku shinshutsu (chūgoku konbini no gyōtai kaihatsu no kagi)*". http://www.jmrlsi.co.jp/oversea/cmt/cmt0905.html. [15 December 2010]

[16] *The Importance of partner Selection in China*, Japan Productivity Center. (http://www.service-js.jp/cms/show_news.php?id=230. [Jun 2010]).

[17] Y. Sato, 2007. Strategy Choices of Convenience Store Chains in China, with Particular Reference to Seven-Eleven and FamilyMart. In Sato Kawakami (eds), *Competition and Cooperation among Asian enterprises in China*. Chosakenkyuu-hokokushu, IDE-JETRO, http://www.ide.go.jp/Japanese/Publish/Download/Report/pdf/2006_04_30_02.pdf. [6 December 2010]

THE PAN-PACIFIC PLAN

Since opening its first store in Taiwan in 1988, FamilyMart has been exploring this market aggressively. Even facing fierce competition in the market, FamilyMart has successfully expanded the store number and grew into the second largest chain. In South Korea, FamilyMart has a strong lead in the industry with approximately 5,000 outlets, which makes the company the country's largest CVS chain. Meanwhile, for FamilyMart and its partner in Thailand, a solid foundation had been built for expanding the chain and further developing their business.

With the successful overseas performance, the total store number of all FamilyMart chains reached 10,000 at the end of 2003. Ueda Junji, the CEO of FamilyMart, announced the "Pan-Pacific Plan", intending to construct a global network of 20,000 stores (approximately 8,000 stores in Japan and 12,000 stores overseas) by 2008.[18] Under this plan, FamilyMart aimed to set up stores in the Chinese market, considered as the main growth driver of the chain in the future. Furthermore, business should be expanded to the US, as a first step to the Western market. In short, the main goal of the Pan-Pacific Plan was to strengthen FamilyMart's competency in the Pan-Pacific region by cooperating with the company's worldwide franchisers and by using the Japanese CVS operation know-how.[19]

CHINA — LAND OF OPPORTUNITIES?

While the Japanese market is approaching saturation, in contrast, the CVS industry in many emerging markets is booming. Among them, China, which is currently the world's second largest economy, is

[18] "Expanding the Pan-Pacific Branch of the Family Tree", FamilyMart, http://www.family.co.jp/english/investor_relations/annual_report/pdf/05_e_03.pdf. [4 January 2010]

[19] "Store Opening Strategy", FamilyMart, 2004, http://www.family.co.jp/english/investor_relations/annual_report/pdf/03_e_06d.pdf. [20 November 2010]

the one with the most potential. Though the average individual consumption level is relatively low, the rapidly growing economy and the huge size of the market have attracted many foreign companies into the Chinese market.

In 1991, the Chinese government opened up the previously restricted retail, finance and construction sectors,[20] triggering an investment boom.[21] China began to gradually remove market-entry barriers and liberalize FDI restrictions after its accession to the WTO in 2001. Retailers were allowed to enter the Chinese market without significant restrictions regarding location. Also, investors were permitted to run all kinds of distribution businesses.[22]

In China, the convenience and discount formats were underdeveloped, not only in rural areas but also in big cities. Food health concerns created strong consumer sentiments about food safety and food origin, giving positive effects on sales of processed food.[23] These factors motivated worldwide retailers to come to China.

After Lawson, another Japanese CVS Chain entered Shanghai in 1996, the CVS industry in China started to grow rapidly and competition became fierce. After Lawson brought the "real CVS operation" into the Chinese market, several new chains appeared in the market with a similar business concept. In 2002, the number of the CVS in Shanghai was 2,000 and it exceeded 5,000 in 2004.[24] Including

---

[20] Before July 1992, FDI in any form was prohibited in the retail industry in China. With the loosening of the restriction, six cities (Beijing, Shanghai, Tianjin, Guangzhou, Qingdao) and five special economic zones were opened to foreign companies for joint ventures with local players, who held at least 51% of the stake.

[21] R. Tan, "Foreign Direct Investment Flows to and from China", *PASCN Discussion Paper No. 99–21.*

[22] China's Policies on FDI: Review and Evaluation, http://www.piie.com/publications/chapters_preview/3810/12iie3810.pdf. [5 January 2011]

[23] K. Chisachi, "*Shijō no hōwa to tatakau konbini ensustoa*" *Nikkei Business Online*, http://business.nikkeibp.co.jp/article/manage/201018/216707/.

[24] I. Kazuya and Y. Akira, 2009, "*Lon, Konbini de chūgoku shinshutsu (chūgoku konbini no gyōtai kaihatsu no kagi)*". http://www.jmrlsi.co.jp/oversea/cmt/cmt0905.html. [20 December 2010]

Lawson, the five main chains in Shanghai occupied more than 90% of the market share, creating serious competition in the CVS industry.[25]

Although the Chinese CVS chains grew quickly, sales per store were relatively low in comparison with those of foreign chains. A lacking ability to develop original goods, an absence of an integrated system, and poor distribution system were some reasons behind this situation. By providing common goods, the local chains fail to differentiate their merchandise from those available in supermarkets, where consumers can purchase the same product for a lower price. Without an integrated system, the Chinese CVS chains can only provide a limited variety of goods, making it difficult to attract customers. Finally, without a well-constructed distribution system, the storage of products (in particular the ready-to-eat items) becomes insufficient, hampering the management of the chains.[26]

When the pioneering foreign CVS chains entered China, Lawson established Shanghai Hualian Lawson Co., Ltd. in 1996 through a joint venture with a local company. Eager to introduce the Japanese CVS concept to the new market, Lawson at first copied the operation model directly from Japan. Although the Japanese concept became very popular in Shanghai, Lawson did not succeed in expanding the chain swiftly. Seven years after the entry, the store number did not reach 100 and the company was in deficit.[27] Reasons for this development were the company's inability reach a profitable scale due to low store numbers, and communication problems with the local staff.

Holding the majority stock of the joint venture, Lawson ran the company with strong leadership. The business structure was very similar to the Japanese one, with the top management consisting of Japanese, and decision-making processes going through the Japanese head office. However, by failing to bring up the chain, in 2001 Lawson modified its strategy and accelerated the degree of localiza-

---

[25] The situation of China's convenience stores (benriten), http://www.news.janjan. jp/world/0610/0610303694/1.php. [October 2010] Shanghai benriten, http://news.xinhuanet.com/fortune/2002–04/26/content_373186.htm. [April 2010].
[26] Y. Sato, *op. cit.*, 2007.
[27] Lawson initially set the goal of achieving 500 stores in five years.

tion. Furthermore, Lawson reduced its stock portion and gave the partner more freedom to lead the business.[28] With the new HRM system designed for the local staff and with the assistance of the Chinese partner, a more localized business model had been adapted and the Lawson chain started growing.[29]

FAMILYMART'S OPERATIONS IN CHINA

Shanghai FamilyMart Co. Ltd. was established in July 2004 after Junji Ueda announced the "Pan-Pacific Plan". The Chinese business started with 25 directly managed stores. After the Chinese government lifted the restrictions on FDI in the end of the year, franchise stores also opened.

To develop its business in Shanghai, FamilyMart established a joint venture with Itochu Cooperation, Taiwan FamilyMart Co. Ltd. and the Ting Hsin International Group. The joint venture was formed to utilize the venture partners' own unique strengths and increase FamilyMart's performance in the Chinese market.

FamilyMart is the brand provider of the alliance. Besides, it also provides the general know-how and system for CVS operations including a computerized information system. Itochu, one of the largest trading companies in Japan, is responsible for the construction and operation of the logistics system in China, while Ting Hsin is in charge for food development and production. Finally, Taiwan FamilyMart plays an extraordinarily important role in the team by managing the supply chain in China. Since Taiwan FamilyMart possesses resources such as manpower, and linguistic and cultural similarities to the Chinese network that are not available to either

---

[28] Japanese Distributors' Entry into China's Markets, Tomohiro Kohara, *Sanken Series* 43, 2008.

[29] Lawson refused to adapt to the local tax rule since the company wanted to bring a pure Japanese CVS management system in the market, thus it had difficulties to build a good relationship with the product suppliers and delivery company. Under the partner's leadership, Shanghai Lawson complied with the custom and this movement was seen as one of the factors that supported the expansion.

FamilyMart or Itochu, many senior executives were sent to Shanghai to provide its experience and take part in the HRM process. Ting Hsin International Group is the largest comprehensive food manufacturer in China, owning the largest instant noodle brand in the world.

Itochu is holding the largest share of the joint venture and is the main leader of the team. Since the company's product distribution extends throughout China, it provides effective infrastructure resources and well-established systems for FamilyMart's needs.[30]

To achieve business success in Shanghai, FamilyMart offers its original products to differentiate the chain from other competitors. In order to ensure that employees provides the "FamilyMart Feel" in stores, they have to attend trainings in FamilyMart's own training centers to deliver the FamilyMart hospitality to the consumers. Other HRM systems such as the Store Staff Qualification System were also imported to China. To share the CVS concept in business developing, FamilyMart created an unrestricted channel between the head office and the franchise stores for communication.

FamilyMart introduced fast food such as sandwiches, bento, onigiri (rice balls) and other Japanese meals like oden. The food served is based on the flavor in Japan and Taiwan with necessary adjustments in order to adapt to the locals. The bakery section in FamilyMart store also became popular. Although there is no such tradition of eating bread in China, it gradually became a new diet habit. To further differentiate itself, FamilyMart targets at the wealthy Chinese and provide them with "Japan-grown" products which became popular among consumers because of its taste, food safety and appearance. Moreover, FamilyMart is planning to establish a domestic company to grow crops for selling agricultural product overseas in 2015.

To quickly introduce the FamilyMart services and products to the Chinese consumers, FamilyMart opened six temporary stores outside the Expo sites using the 2010 Shanghai Expo as an exposure opportunity for the 70 million people who were expected to visit the exhibition.

---

[30] Japanese Distributors' Entry into China's Markets, Tomohiro Kohara, Sanken Series 43, 2008.

In Shanghai, FamilyMart targets two kinds of store locations: the traditional "street-facing" store and the off-street "new market" such as in office buildings, hospitals and on university campuses. Also, based on a strategic alliance with Shanghai Metro, FamilyMart plans to increase store opening inside the subway stations as well.[31]

To supply the products for the expanding chain in Shanghai, a business center was built up, combining a plant for fast food products and a logistics center, capable of handling all temperature ranges. All this gives FamilyMart a solid foundation for its future expansions in Shanghai.

MORE TARGETS IN CHINA

In 2006, FamilyMart entered the southern Chinese City, Guangzhou, before it spread to Suzhou in 2007 with its joint venture partners from Shanghai. According to the motto "things that work in Shanghai will work in the whole China", FamilyMart has planned to fully utilize the experience it gained from the operations in Shanghai. Centered in Shanghai, Guangzhou and Suzhou, FamilyMart has been aggressively expanding the chain.

Having focused on the urban areas, FamilyMart announced to enter Sichuan and to accelerate its expansion not only in first tier cities but also in some second tier cities, in order to realize its expansion goal to increase the store number tenfold from 450 in the end of 2010 to 4,500 by 2015.

CHINESE CHALLENGES

Although the business is growing at a steady pace, more challenges exist for FamilyMart to further expand the chain in China. China's poor infrastructure is the biggest obstacle the chain has to face in the market. Since products have to be distributed to the convenience store every day, distribution plays an important role in the CVS industry. However, in a market that lacks well-functioning infrastructure,

---

[31] FamilyMart Annual Report 2010.

facilities and logistics, FamilyMart has to acquire the distribution facilities before it moves to new areas.

FamilyMart also faces regulatory problems. Under the Chinese government's growing emphasis on product safety and environmental regulation, the chain has to acquire many complicated permissions and develop store facilities that match these rules in order to operate the business. It can therefore be very time consuming for a chain to understand the regulations before the business starts. Local business norms such as the transaction rule[32] and the value-added taxation system which is different from the one in Japan also urges FamilyMart to develop appropriate procedures to fit the local requirements.

In order to operate the business smoothly in the Chinese market, enterprises have to deal with many government entities, which have influence over the related industry. In addition, regulations of the central government are not always enforced at the local levels, or there may be inconsistencies in enforcing the regulations. While local companies might be used to these circumstances, and know how to communicate and negotiate with the government, it is a big challenge for a Japanese company such as FamilyMart.

FamilyMart also faces difficulties staffing its Chinese locations with a workforce that is experience enough to establish a CVS chain in a new market and to assist the expansion goals in China.[33] Although China has a vast population, foreign companies usually face talent shortages both when they enter the market and when they manage

---

[32] The transaction rules in China differ from those in Japan. Also, it is considered a threat to the spread of CVS franchising since under the regulation, most of the benefits go to the franchisers and the franchisees' margin is squeezed. In China, regardless of the purchasing volume, manufacturers hold strong powers that enable them to fix the shipping price. The competition is very fierce in the Chinese retail market and thus the retailers tend to make very small margins, but in China, they are allowed to return the unsold goods in any condition. Besides, the large buyers receive benefits from the manufacturers such as offered a cash rebate instead of discount, co-sponsor for some events and get the salesman dispatched to stores.

[33] Long Ke (2007). Chinese Job Dilemma: Labor surplus and talent shortage, *Fujitsu Economic Review*, 11(1). http://jp.fujitsu.com/group/fri/report/economic-review/200701/page11.html. [15 December 2010]

the business. To operate a franchise chain and to convey the "FamilyMart Feel" in China, communication with the local workforce is essential. However, language and culture differences represent serious obstacles for transferring CVS operation concepts. This poses as big challenges since a good communication between FamilyMart and its employees is important to maintain a high quality store management.

As the economy grew, rents cost in Shanghai began to outpace earnings on the low margin goods and services sold at convenience stores. This had a strong impact on profitability. High rent cost could limit floor area, leading to less merchandise variety, and inhibit the network's prospects for rapid expansion. There are even cases where a convenience store went bankrupt due to the rise in the rent.[34] Although lacking such experience, FamilyMart has to balance between rent and floor area, while expanding the store numbers at the same time.

In the highly competitive Chinese market, FamilyMart has to compete with both the local and foreign chains. To differentiate itself from rivals, FamilyMart emphasizes on "non-tangible" strengths, like offering the FamilyMart hospitality through high quality services to its customers. The "FamilyMart Feel" strategy seems to work in China at the current stage. However, with the expansion of other Japanese chains, which also provide comparable levels of service, and with fiercer competition in the market, can loyalty really be built among the price sensitive Chinese consumers through branding the "FamilyMart Feel?"

Although the Chinese market offers opportunities, it proved more difficult than FamilyMart had thought. Barriers existed not only at the time of penetrating the market but also at every level of operation. However, FamilyMart sees China as the future growth driver and is planning to enter into the Sichuan market in 2012, expanding the chain to inner China. Although the Chinese market plays a vital part within FamilyMart's ambitious global growth strategy, reaching the ambitious goal of 25,000 stores in 2015 will be a big challenge.

---

[34] N. Tomomi, "*Konbini gyōkai no genjō to kadai*" *Kabushikigaisha tōre keiei kenkyūsho* http://www.tbr.co.jp/pdf/sensor/sen_a101.pdf. [10 January 2010]

QUESTIONS

1. Why does FamilyMart choose joint venture as its basic entry mode to overseas market?
2. What are the strategies used by FamilyMart to expand its chains to overseas markets? What are the advantages?
3. What challenges does the Chinese market provide for foreign companies attempting to enter the market?
4. As an Asian company, does FamilyMart focus on different aspects compared to Western firms when entering overseas markets?

BIBLIOGRAPHY

Alan H. and FAS China staff, 2010, Spending on food surges while distribution remains a challenge, GAIN Report: CH0801. [online] Available at: http://www.morgenevan.com/pages/reports/China_F&B_Sector.pdf [10 December 2010]

ChinaRetailNews.com, "FamilyMart to open 100 new stores in Shanghai in 2010". China Retail News. [online] Available at: <http://www.chinaretailnews.com/2010/03/09/3415-FamilyMart-to-open-100 -new-stores-in-shanghai-in-2010/> [25 January 2011]

FamilyMart, 2005, Annual report 2005 [Online] Available at:http://www. family.co.jp/english/investor_relations/annual_report/2005.html

FamilyMart. FamilyMart opens 15,000 store in Pan-Pacific network. *FamilyMart new releases.* (Last updated Oct 11, 2006), http://www.family.co.jp/english/news_releases/061011.html [25 January 2001]

FamilyMart. FamilyMart sets up joint venture in Guangzhou. *FamilyMart new releases.* (Last updated Oct 11, 2006), http://www.family.co.jp/english/news_releases/061011.html [26 January 2011]

Fujitsu Webpage, [online] Available at: http://business.nikkeibp.co.jp/article/manage/20101018/216707/ [10 December 2010]

Ka Takashi, 2007, "Chūgoku ni okeru rōdōryoku kajō to jinzai fusoku no jirenma" (「中国における労働力過剰と人材不足のジレンマ」)

Morgen, Evan & Company, Inc. (2006) *The Chinese food and beverage sector.* http://www.morgenevan.com/pages/reports/China_F&B_Sector. pdf [5 December 2010]

Nikkei ryūtsū kigyō no chūgoku tenkai: (Sekai shijō) he no sannyū senryaku) Waseda daigaku sangyō keiei kenyŭūsho (「日系流通企業の中国展開：「世界市場」への参入戦略」早稲田大学産業経営研究所) Waseda Business Review 4:3.

Purkayastha, D, 2008, *Multinational Retail Chains & the China opportunity*. ICMR: 208-102-1

Reuters. *FamilyMart to stay US, China pace picks up. Reuters.* (Last updated Nov 25, 2010) http://www.reuters.com/article/2010/11/25/idUK-TOE6AO05U20101125 [26 January 2001]

The Yomiuri Shinbun. FamilyMart to export agriculture goods to China. Daily Yomiuri Online. (Last updated Oct 4, 2011), http://www.asian-ewsnet.net/home/news.php?id=14742 [25 January 2011]

Alibaba: Facing its Thieves

Xiaozhou Wu

INTRODUCTION

Jack Ma, the Founder and Chairman of Alibaba Group was frowning in concentration at his office of the Alibaba's headquarter in Hangzhou. It seemed that this year would not be a good year for the company. According to the Chinese zodiac theory, it was a year of misfortune for Alibaba. Chinese believe in 12-year-cycle barriers, which means, after every 12-years there would be a tough point in life: one faces the adolescence problem at the age of 12, the problem of getting adapted to the society at the age of 24 and getting matured at the age of 36. At those turning points one would be confronted with more barriers than in other years. Just this year, the 12th anniversary of Alibaba, many problems broke out at the same time. Many of its customers in the past two years committed fraud and caused a large loss to the company.

ALIBABA IN THE NEWS

The secretary came into Ma's office and extended her greetings to Jack Ma. "Sir Ma, I have a magazine here. The feature is about Alibaba" said the secretary politely.

"Put it there. I will read it later." answered Jack Ma.

After checking his mailbox, he began scanning the main points in the article:

"Alibaba: the new e-commerce empire. Today our feature column gives insights into the famous Chinese enterprise".[1]

The Alibaba Group and its companies

The Alibaba group has its headquarter in Hangzhou, P.R. China and offices in Hongkong, Europe, India, Japan, Korea and the U.S. with more than 25,000 employees in around 70 cities. In the following, we give a rough outline of the group's companies and services.

Alibaba.com is the world's largest business-to-business (B2B) marketplace where buyers and suppliers, usually small and medium enterprises from more than 240 countries and regions can communicate and trade with each other. The way its members can trade on Alibaba's platform is very convenient. Membership for suppliers is free. They can get a website for displaying all their products. Buyers can search products on Alibaba.com, find product suppliers, get contacted with them and make a trade. Suppliers in turn can also search for buyers, negotiate with them and make the transaction.

Alibaba has specialized marketplaces for its customers. The international marketplace, www.alibaba.com, is mainly for suppliers who export their products to the world, while the China market, www.alibaba.com.cn, is for suppliers exporting their products to China or making trade within China. In the international marketplace over 4.4 million registered members trade on this platform, with the majority of members (24%) being located in the USA. In the China marketplace, over 23.2 million registered members are from China. The majority comes from the Guangdong Province, Zhejiang Province and other strong economic areas along the east coast. Furthermore, Alibaba provides a website, www.alibaba.co.jp for customers in the Japanese market.

(Continued)

---

[1] Adapted from Alibaba.com, "Company Overview": http://news.alibaba.com/specials/aboutalibaba/aligroup/index.html and Alibaba.com, "Financial Reports": http://ir.alibaba.com/ir/home/financial_reports.htm. More detailed History can be found in Exhibit 1.

(Continued)

The paying members exceeded one million at the end of 2010 and more than 61 million users were registered. There are more than 8.5 million storefronts.

Aliexpress (www.aliexpress.com) offers a transaction-based global wholesale platform aiming at small buyers, seeking fast shipments of small quantities of goods.

Taobao Marketplace is the largest consumer-to-consumer (C2C) online marketplace in China. There are more than 800 million product listings and more than 370 million registered users on its marketplace.

Taobao Mall is China's leading business-to-consumer (B2C) online marketplace in China. It takes up around half of the share of China's B2C online retail market. 70,000 international and Chinese brands from 50,000 merchants can be found on the website.

eTao, which was launched jointly with Microsoft, is a leading search engine for product and merchant information in China. eTao helps customers to make purchase decisions efficiently and to identify low-cost, high-quality merchandise on the Internet.

Alipay is an online escrow payment platform. It provides a user-friendly and transaction- guaranty model for business partners to make and receive online payments. In China, about 65 financial institutions are involved in this online escrow paying system, for example China Merchants Bank, China Construction Bank, Agricultural Bank of China and Industrial and Commercial Bank of China. The customers "deposit" their payment to Alipay and hand over the payment to the sellers after the customers received the products. According to Alibaba, until the end of 2010 there were more than 550 million registered users and about 8.5 million transactions daily.

Alibaba Cloud Computing is an advanced data-centric cloud computing service. It aims at providing clients with an integrated suite of internet-based computing services, which include e-commerce data mining, high-speed processing of e-commerce data, and data customization.

(Continued)

(Continued)

In 2005 Alibaba Group acquired China Yahoo! It is well known as China's leading Internet service, offering E-mail services, a search engine and news portals.

Investor Relations

In the board of directors, Yahoo!Inc. takes up 40% of Alibaba Group's shares. 31.7% are owned by the founder Jack Ma and his management team. Softbank has 29.3% of Alibaba's shares. Taobao Marketplace, Taobao Mall, eTao, Alibaba Cloud Computing and China Yahoo! are wholly owned by Alibaba Group. Alipay is an affiliate of the Alibaba Group. From 1999 to 2000 Alibaba accepted venture capital of US$5 million from Transpac Capital, Investor AB, Goldman Sachs, Fidelity and other risk investment institutions. In 2000 Softbank invested US$20 million. Meanwhile, Masayoshi Son, CEO of Softbank, and Peter Sutherland, Chairman of Goldman Sachs, joined as board of advisors.[2]

Alibaba's acquisition of China Yahoo! began in 2005. China Yahoo! took 40% of Alibaba's shares for US$1 billion. In return, Alibaba acquired China Yahoo!'s assets including its website and search engine.[3] In November 2007, Alibaba.com successfully made its first initial public offering at the price of HK$13.5 on the Hong Kong Stock Exchange. The IPO raised in total US$1.7 billion.

Financial Highlights[4]

In 2010 the revenue of Alibaba.com grew to 5.56 billion RMB, increasing by 43% from the last year. Compared to 2007,

(Continued)

---

[2] Alibaba.com, "Company Overview": http://news.alibaba.com/specials/aboutalibaba/aligroup/index.html.

[3] Asia Times Online, "Sino-foreign deals attract attention": http://www.atimes.com/atimes/China/GH13Ad02.html.

[4] Alibaba.com, "Annual Report 2010": http://ir.alibaba.com/ir/home/financial_reports.htm.

(Continued)

revenues grew by nearly 50%. The basic earnings per share reached HK $ 33 Cents. The profit attributable to equity owners reached 1.47 billion RMB. In the international market, revenues reached 3.3 billion RMB, 58.2% of total revenue for Alibaba.com, while in the Chinese market, the revenue reached 1.8 billion RMB, 34.1% of total revenue for Alibaba.com. Compared to 2009, EBITA rose by 52% from around 1.0 billion RMB to 1.6 billion RMB in 2010. The net profit grew by 43% up to 1.4 billion RMB.[5]

Alibaba's Competitors

As a B2B company, Alibaba.com faces new competitors virtually every day. The threshold is relatively low and copycats can easily imitate Alibaba's business concepts and set up an own website. However, it is not a very easy task to attract customers and earn reputation as a B2B website. Although Alibaba takes up the main market power, there are always small companies, which take part in the competition, for example www.globalsources.com, or www.made-in-China.com. However, the revenue of Alibaba still amounted to 70% of the Chinese online B2B companies' revenue in the fourth quarter of 2010. Global competitors include www.Made-from-India.com, www.exportnation.com, www.tradeindia.com, www.hellotrade.com.[6]

Another threat to the B2B business comes from the existence of worldwide or regional trade fairs, which can be considered as a substitute for online trading and which are immune to the different types of online fraud.

Because of the wide diversification of Alibaba Group, its competitors and potential competitors cover every aspects of internet

(Continued)

---

[5] Exhibit 2 shows selected financial and operational data for the Alibaba Group. (See Appendix)

[6] The main competitive rivals within the industry are demonstrated in Exhibit 3. (See Appendix)

(Continued)

business. Some of the major competitors in the area of B2B and B2C are Baidu, Tencent and eBay. Baidu is a search engine that provides a wide range of services, for example among others a Chinese language search engine, online community encyclopedias (similar to Wikipedia), discussion forums, Baidu Map (services similar to those of Google Map), Baidu Space (services similar to Facebook).

Tencent's instant messenger QQ (similar to Skype) is the most used instant messenger (IM) and has the world's largest online community. At the end of 2010 647.6 million users had a Tencent QQ account.[7] It is the number three behind the biggest internet companies Google and Amazon. Paipai.com, a C2C auction website, was founded by Tencent in 2006. Meanwhile it also launched Soso.com, a search engine website and Tenpay, an online payment system similar to Alipay."

Reading about the growing number of competitors, Jack Ma found himself concerned about the threats looming on the horizon. However, he felt proud about the size and importance his company gained through the years. He leaned back in his chair and began strolling back in time in his mind.

THE BIRTH OF ALIBABA.COM

Thinking of the past was always a good way for Jack Ma to distract himself from the thorny issues on such a day. Sometimes he would be delighted from the bottom of his heart when he thought about the early years of Alibaba, its birth, its growth and its maturity.

In the 1990s, there were only a few people in China with access to the Internet. Jack Ma was no exeption. In 1995 he was appointed by the province government to be a translator for a Chinese investment project on a US highway. It was his first time to get in touch

[7] Tencent, "Annual Report 2010": http://www.tencent.com/en-us/ir/reports.shtml.

with the Internet and he found that there was astonishingly very little online information about Chinese businesses.

He decided this should change and put some information about Chinese companies online. After he had created a website about a Chinese translation service company at 9 a.m., he received already four emails at 12 a.m. He was so excited about this idea and tried to attract more companies on his website. He realized that there was a great information asymmetry between Chinese small companies and international purchasers.[8]

In 1995, Ma founded his first Internet company, China Pages. Two years later, after he joined the China International Electronic Commerce Center, he and his partners founded several commercial websites. With the economic boom in China, there was more and more demand for the Internet. E-Commerce burgeoned. By the end of 1998 that he and his 17 colleagues set up a new website, Alibaba. com, the group was officially launched in 1999 in Hangzhou with a capital of RMB 500,000.[9]

But why did Jack Ma name his company after the famous character from the Arabic literature? Once he was sitting in a coffee shop in San Francisco and thought about a name for his company. In order to prove that it was known to everyone, he asked a waitress about her thoughts on the word "Alibaba". She answered without hesitation "Open, Sesame".[10]

In the story, Alibaba is a kind and clever person. When he says "Open sesame!", the gate leading to a treasure opens. Jack Ma hoped that his company would have the characteristics like Alibaba: opening up the sesame for small businesses in China or all around the world.[11]

---

[8] Alibaba.com: http://info.china.alibaba.com/news/detail/v0-d1000407182.html.

[9] Sheng Hua, "Ma Yun Chuan Qi (Legend of Jack Ma)", Chinese Economy Press, Aug 1st 2009.

[10] Alibaba.com, "INTERVIEW-China's Alibaba taking aim at U.S. market.", http://news.alibaba.com/article/detail/alibaba/100093555-1-interview-china%2527s-alibaba-taking-aim-u.s.html.

[11] Sheng Hua, "Ma Yun Chuan Qi (Legend of Jack Ma)", Chinese Economy Press, Aug 1st 2009.

THE RISE OF ALIBABA.COM

It is always the first step that is troublesome. The Internet was not very popular in China. The newly born Alibaba had to offer its service free of charge, in order to convince its potential customers to get acquainted with this new form of trading. More and more customers came to make a trade on the website. Till January 2000, the number of members had reached 500,000, although the dotcom bubble burst and a lot of e-commerce companies went into bankruptcy.

In the same year, the company began to offer a new service, Gold Supplier, a premium membership for Chinese suppliers on Alibaba. com. As a Gold Supplier, the supplier can acquire a large range of service provided by Alibaba. On Alibaba's website, Gold Suppliers are displayed with a golden icon and a large number of buyers prefer trading with them because the icon was supposed to demonstrate their authenticity. The Gold Supplier can have contact to buyers immediately, while normal members have to wait for seven days. They can customize the company profile with easy tools and display unlimited products, while normal members can only display 50 products. A Gold Supplier is listed with first level priority and has an exclusive access to buyers. Furthermore, a Gold Supplier can read real time statistical reports on their personal online performance.[12]

For receiving a Gold Supplier membership, authentication and verification processes executed by a third party security provider are necessary. The service fee for Gold Suppliers is not charged per trade but is priced at 60,000 RMB–80,000 RMB per year. For companies from Mainland China an application for a Gold Supplier is mandatory. In 2007 and 2008 the Gold Supplier status was also made available to suppliers in Hongkong and Taiwan. Alibaba began charging the member fee at the end of 2001 and became profitable in the same year. The Gold Supplier strategy is Alibaba's main strategy for its international market on www.alibaba.com.

International TrustPass members, a much cheaper paid membership was then introduced, in order to serve exporters outside China.

---

[12] Alibaba.com, "Gold Supplier": http://ggs.alibaba.com/

For the domestic market Alibaba utilized a similar strategy. China TrustPass was introduced to its domestic market, which was charged at 2,300 RMB per year and later raised to 2,800 RMB per year.

In July 2002, keyword services were launched as premium service on Alibaba's international marketplace, generating another profit model for the company. It allows Gold Suppliers to be ranked higher in the search results by purchasing certain keywords referring to their products. Since buyers tend to view only the 1st page of search results, this is quite a useful function for a supplier.[13] Alibaba.com brought the keyword services also to its domestic markets in 2005.

Some members found it quite difficult to get in touch with potential contract partners. They claimed that there should be some software for instant messaging, which facilitates online trading. Therefore, in November 2003, TradeManager (in Chinese *AliWangwang*) was introduced. With this free instant messenger the suppliers and buyers can chat and deal with each other online.[14]

Until the end of 2007, 27.6 million users were registered at Alibaba.com, while at the end of 2006 the number had been only 19.8 million. In the same period, the number of paying members increased from around 219,000 to 306,000. The revenue of 2007 reached 2,162,757 RMB, increasing by 59% compared to 2006.[15]

In the following years, many more paid services were designed for its members: The premium placements, costing 5,300 RMB per month in the domestic market enable members to have their product advertisement displayed on the right side of the search result page.[16] Export-to-China (2008) was introduced for non-Chinese SME companies, giving them support for their business with China's domestic

---

[13] Alibaba.com, "ANNOUNCEMENT OF ANNUAL RESULTS FOR THE YEAR ENDED DECEMBER 31, 2007": http://img.alibaba.com/ir/download/200803/Announcement_ENG.pdf.

[14] Alibaba.com, "TradeManager": http://trademanager.alibaba.com/.

[15] Alibaba.com, "Annual Report 2007": http://ir.alibaba.com/ir/home/financial_reports.htm.

[16] Alibaba.com, "ANNOUNCEMENT OF ANNUAL RESULTS FOR THE YEAR ENDED DECEMBER 31, 2007": http://img.alibaba.com/ir/download/200803/Announcement_ENG.pdf.

market.[17] In 2009, PPC (pay per click), an online advertising bidding service, was introduced.[18]

BUILDING UP AN E-EMPIRE

Ma stood up and looked out of one of his office windows. In front of him he saw a place, which used to be a wasteland a few years ago but now turned out to be full of office buildings, cars and white-collar workers. The rapid growth of the Chinese economy has given Chinese entrepreneurs more opportunities for diversification. For Jack Ma it was certain that he would not give up any opportunity for Alibaba to become a virtual empire.

In May 2003, Alibaba entered into the C2C-business area by the founding of Taobao, a consumer e-commerce platform. In 2010, Alibaba and Microsoft Corporation jointly launched eTao, an online shopping web search service, in order to challenge the strong position of Baidu, a major player in the Chinese online search market.[19] At the same time, Jack Ma created a cross-business team, consisting of senior managers from Taobao, Alipay, Alibaba Cloud computing and China Yahoo! to carry out the so-called "'Big Taobao' strategy". This strategy focused on positioning Taobao as a central e-commerce platform, providing consumers and businesses with a broad range of e-commerce services.[20] This strategy was the starting point to not only establish Alibaba in the field of B2B, but also in the fields of B2C and C2C.

During the last years Alibaba invested in many other Internet-related fields. Jack Ma made invested in Koubei.com. Koubei.com was founded in Hangzhou in 2004 and has become one of China's

[17] Alibaba.com, "Export-to-China": http://www.alibaba.com/activities/export_to_china/export_to_china_get_in.html.
[18] Exhibit 4 gives a product overview.
[19] The Wall Street Journal, "Alibaba, Microsoft Team Up on Chinese Search Site": http://online.wsj.com/article/SB10001424052748703440004575547284215718978.html.
[20] Alibaba.com, "Company Overview": http://news.alibaba.com/specials/aboutalibaba/aligroup/index.html.

leading online classified listing and community websites. Besides posting classified ads, its users can exchange on favorite restaurants, movies and songs, or search for jobs and apartments etc.[21] The company later merged with China Yahoo! to form Yahoo! Koubei.

At the beginning of 2007, Alisoft, which focuses on business software development, was launched. The company devotes itself to provide SME with convenient e-commerce software in order to manage their businesses. Its services include customer relationship management, inventory management, sales force management, financial tools and marketing information management.[22] In 2009, Alisoft was merged with Alibaba R&D Institute.

Also in 2007, an online advertising exchange platform for trading online advertising inventory was launched. On Alimama, Chinese web publishers can offer online advertisement positions to Chinese advertisers.[23] Alimama was integrated with Taobao, in September 2008.

Finally, in 2009, the year of Alibaba's 10-year anniversary, Alibaba Cloud Computing was founded. Alibaba Group thus became a virtual empire, serving business customers, private customers and offering every imaginable multimedia service.

The Fraud Crisis

Back at the desk, Jack Ma held two resignation letters in his hands: one from his CEO David Wei and one from his COO Elvis Li. After a big scandal broke out in the group, Jack Ma and the board of directors were facing a hard decision on whether they should accept the resignation or not. However, they decided that someone has to take

---

[21] Alibaba.com, "Alibaba.com Makes Strategic Investment in Koubei.com": http://resources.alibaba.com/article/20375/Alibaba_com_Makes_Strategic_Investment_in_Koubei_com.htm.

[22] Alibaba.com, "Alibaba Group Launches Business Software Company": http://www.alibaba.com/aboutalibaba/aligroup/press_releases070108.html.

[23] Alibaba.com, "Alibaba Group Launches Online Advertising Exchange Company Alimama": http://www.alibaba.com/aboutalibaba/aligroup/press_releases071120.html.

the responsibility for this scandal. Otherwise the aftereffect of this event was too dreadful to contemplate for Alibaba.

Trust can certainly be considered as one of the most important factors for companies who offer online trading. If an e-commerce company loses its trust, it means that it damages its reputation and its whole business.

How did fraudulent suppliers commit their crimes? A typical case: Suppose Customer A demands a quantity of certain products. Customer A looks for a Gold Supplier on Alibaba's website. In the end, he finds supplier B and gets contacted with B. A is required by B to submit a certain amount of money as "deposit". After paying, A would not receive the products and would then find out that he cannot get in touch with B again and does not receive the ordered products.

Complaints about fraudulent suppliers have been continuing to appear. As a response, the escrow system Alipay had been introduced to Alibaba.com in 2005, although its services were only offered to Chinese businesses and individuals. In 2007, however, Alipay additionally started to provide cross-border payments services. Chinese buyers could make purchases with the Chinese currency for goods that are offered in foreign currencies from partner merchant websites outside China. For that, the escrow system withdraws the buyer's payment to exchange it into the foreign currency, which is then transferred to the account of the international seller.[24]

Despite Alibaba's efforts to prevent fraud, there are still many loopholes. For example many customers claimed that only a few Gold Suppliers accept payments *via* the escrow system because of higher handling fees.

Many of its users also complained online that Alibaba does not do enough against scammers and is not taking responsibility for the occurring frauds, apart from deleting the accounts of fraudulent users.

Another reason for the online fraud problem has its origin in the aftermath of the financial crisis from 2008. Because of the weakening of global economies, Alibaba had to lower the membership fee for

---

[24] Alipay.com, "Cross-Border Payment Service Model": http://market.alipay.com/ospay/outboundBusiness/Benefits_for_International_Merchants.html.

Gold Suppliers in order to attract more customers and increase the revenues. Furthermore, Alibaba started to become negligent on the authentication process of its members. Consequently, fraudulent activities increased.

In 2011, Alibaba found that about 2,326 of its Gold Suppliers committed fraud in 2009 and 2010, accounting for 1.1% (2009) and 0.8% (2010) of all Gold Suppliers. According to the company, the average compensation claim per fraud amounted to US$1,200. After admitting the fraud scandal in public, Alibaba paid US$1.7 million to the victims. One day after the announcement, the stock price of Alibaba dropped by around 8.6% and Morgan Stanley downgraded Alibaba's shares from "overweight" to "equal-weight".[25]

In the end, the reputation of Alibaba was clearly damaged. CEO David Wei and COO Elvis Lee resigned to take the responsibility for the scandals. Jonathan Lu was then appointed as CEO of Alibaba.com.

Alibaba has already been taking various measures against fraud in recent years. But every measure has its own drawback. The safe trading class on one of Alibaba's websites provides the readers with how to distinguish genuine traders from scammers. However, this is quite time consuming and the website cannot cover every aspect of preventing a fraud. A significant measure was taken in the second half of 2010, when Alibaba decided to have factory audits being undertaken for Chinese suppliers. These audits are performed by Intertek, a testing, inspection and certification company. However, of course, this turned out to be quite time consuming — taking three month for inspecting only 2,000 suppliers of Alibaba.

AN EMAIL FROM JACK MA

Thinking of the fraud issues, Jack Ma felt tired and almost discouraged. But suddenly his face lit up and he said to his secretary who poured tea

---

[25] Bloomberg, "Alibaba Shares Tumble After Fraud Leads To CEO Departure": http://www.bloomberg.com/news/2011-02-22/alibaba-com-downgraded-by-morgan-stanley-after-ceo-wei-resigns.html.

into a cup on his desk: "It is really not a big deal! Not bad but good! Not a disaster but quite oppositely an opportunity for us." While the secretary was still wondering what to respond, he continued to explain.

"You certainly know the famous Chinese proverb, 塞翁失马, 焉知非福 (A setback may turn out to be a blessing in disguise)? For us the good news in disguise is that this year the scandals have taught us to respond and reform. We are at a milestone, and we should really think about the next one."

"Yes. I guess you are right about this", said the secretary with a lowered voice and gave the cup carefully to Jack Ma. "Chairman Ma, I am going to brew another pot of tea." Ma nodded and she went out. The office turned again into silence and Jack Ma started to write on his computer.

Writing personal emails was always his favorite way to communicate with his staffs. Thus on the next day, when all the staffs were back to office, they received an email from their CEO Jack Ma.

Fellow Aliren:[26]

As we have announced today, the B2B board of directors has accepted the resignations of B2B CEO David Wei and COO Elvis Lee. Additionally, former senior VP of B2B HR Kangming Deng has resigned his post as Chief People Officer of Alibaba Group in acceptance of responsibility and will be demoted to a different post.

Several months ago, we discovered that some of our B2B China Gold Supplier (CGS) members were suspected of fraudulent activity. What made it shocking was evidence indicating that certain members of the CGS sales team knowingly allowed, or in some cases even helped, these fraudulent companies join the Alibaba.com marketplace.

[...]

Any tolerance of this type of affront to business ethics and company values is a crime against the rest of our customers and

---

(Continued)

[26] *Aliren* refers in Chinese to Alibaba's employees.

(*Continued*)

Aliren who remain honest. We must take measures to safeguard the values of Alibaba! All the colleagues who were directly or indirectly involved must be held responsible; more importantly, B2B's management team must assume primary responsibility. We have already terminated the storefronts of all 2,326 CGS members suspected of fraud, and we have asked law enforcement authorities to assist us in our investigation.

Since the day that Alibaba was established, pursuit of profit has never been our main goal. We have no interest in turning the company into a mere money-making machine. Rather, we have long held firm to our mission of "making it easy to do business anywhere." When we say "customer first," we mean that we'd rather sacrifice growth than do anything that would jeopardize our customers' interests, much less be a part of any blatant fraud.

Over this past month, I've experienced a lot of torment, a lot of frustration, a lot of anger...

This is the pain we suffer as we develop, a price that we pay as part of our growth, and it hurts! But we have no choice. It is not possible for us to be mistake-free; we may from time to time commit errors of judgment, but we will absolutely not err by compromising our principles. If we do not face up to reality and find the courage to take painful action, Alibaba will no longer be Alibaba and our pursuit of our 102-year dream and mission will become nothing but a joke!

This world does not need another Internet company, much less another company that can make money;

What this world needs is a company that is more open, more transparent, more sharing, more responsible, more global;

What this world needs is a company that is grounded in society, serves the interests of society, and accepts the responsibilities of society;

What this world needs is a culture, a soul, a belief and an acceptance of obligation. Because these are the only things that will allow us to go further, do better, act with confidence on the challenging path of entrepreneurship.

(*Continued*)

(Continued)

What comforted me is learning that the overwhelming majority of our CGS sales colleagues upheld their principles in the face of temptation. To these colleagues, I salute you! More importantly, we thank the colleagues who have the courage to stand firm and fight against what is wrong. From their actions we witnessed the courage and power of upholding integrity and principles. In them we see Alibaba's future and hope! And we need more Aliren like them! Those who do the extraordinary must assume extraordinary responsibilities!

The resignations of David and Elvis are tremendous losses to the company. For me this is extremely sad and hurtful. But I think their willingness as Aliren to step up and accept responsibility is most admirable. On behalf of the company, I want to express my sincere gratitude to the both of them for their unrelenting dedication and contribution to the company.

[…]

This is an era full of promises and an era that no one wants to miss out on. Only through holding onto our ideals and our principles will we be able to become the pride of this era!

If not now? When?

If not me? Who?

Jack Ma[27]

QUESTIONS

1. What solutions can the company develop to avoid similar problems in the future?
2. How can a company secure business ethics for their own staff and for their customers?
3. How important is the role of the leader in a company crisis like this? Does Jack Ma have a Chinese leadership style?

[27] AllThingsD.com, "Chairman Jack Ma's Internal Email on Alibaba.com Management Shakeup": http://allthingsd.com/20110221/alibaba-group-jack-mas-internal-email-on-alibaba-com-management-shakeup/

APPENDIX

Exhibit 1.   History of Alibaba group.[28]

1999	Alibaba.com is founded in Hangzhou.
	Official Launch of Alibaba.com in Hong Kong.
1999–2000	Venture capital of US$ 25 million is raised.
2000	Launch of Gold Supplier membership (for Chinese exporters)
2001	Launch of International TrustPass (for exporters outside China).
2002	The group reaches profitability.
	Launch of China TrustPass (for domestic Chinese trade).
	Launch of Keyword Ranking Services in the international market.
2003	Taobao is founded.
	Launch of TradeManager (Instant Messenger).
2004	Launch of Alipay.
2005	Takeover of China Yahoo!
	Launch of Keyword Ranking Services in the Chinese market
2006	Investment in Koubei.com.
2007	Launch of brand advertisement in the Chinese market.
	Introduction of Gold Supplier membership to the Hong Kong market.
	Alibaba enters the Japanese market.
	Launch of Alisoft.
	Launch of Gold exhibition space in the domestic market.
	Small Business Commercial Credit Service.
	IPO of Alibaba.com.
	Launch of Alimama.
2008	Introduction of Taobao Mall.
	Koubei.com merges with China Yahoo! under the name of Yahoo! Koubei.
	Alimama is integrated with Taobao.
	Alibaba Group R&D Institute is established.
	Alibaba.com Japan is founded as a joint venture between Alibaba.com and Softbank.

(Continued)

---

[28] Parts are from Alibaba.com, "Company Overview": http://news.alibaba.com/specials/aboutalibaba/aligroup/index.html and Alibaba.com.

Exhibit 1.   (*Continued*)

	Launch of personal TrustPass Membership in the Chinese market.
	Launch of Gold Supplier Membership in the Taiwanese market.
	Launch of Export-to-China Service (for exporters to China).
	Launch of Alibaba PPC, named Wangxiaobao, a Keyword Bidding System.
	Alisoft merges with Alibaba Group's R&D Institute.
	Big Taobao Strategy is formulated.
	Launch of Alibaba Cloud Computing.
2010	Creation of a cross business team to perform the Big Taobao Strategy.
	Launch of Aliexpress.
2011	The fraud scandal is publicly admitted. The CEO of Alibaba.com and COO of the Alibaba Group resign.

Exhibit 2. Financial and operational highlights of Alibaba.com (2006–2010).[29]

	2006	2007	2008	2009	2010
Revenue (RMB)	1,363,862	2,162,757	3,001,194	3,874,700	5,557,600
International marketplace	991,869	1,535,156	1,883,966	2,406,804	3,238,243
China Gold Suppliers	967,858	1,502,331	1,842,884	2,344,475	3,148,498
Global Gold Suppliers	24,011	32,825	41,082	62,329	89,745
China marketplace	371,993	615,062	1,094,059	1,414,897	1,893,899
China TrustPass	363,653	594,098	1,026,883	1,344,029	1,812,991
Other Revenue	2,340	20,964	67,176	70,868	80,908
Others	—	11,539	23,169	53,027	425,444
EBITA	291,388	1,149,444	1,364,820	1,176,419	1,706,457
Profit attributable to equity owners (RMB)	219,938	967,795	1,205,186	1,073,000	1,469,500
Earnings per share (HK$)	4.46 Cents	20.41 Cents	26.74 Cents	22.81 Cents	33 Cents
Registered Users	19,764,226	27,599,959	38,075,335	47,732,916	61,801,281
International Marketplace	3,115,153	4,405,557	7,914,630	11,578,247	18,024,993
China Marketplace	16,649,073	23,194,402	30,160,705	36,154,669	43,776,288
Storefronts	2,072,765	2,956,846	4,614,250	6,819,984	8,544,544
International Marketplace	514,891	697,563	966,747	1,400,326	1,696,905
China Marketplace	1,557,874	2,259,283	3,648,503	5,419,658	6,874,639
Paying members	219,098	305,545	432,031	615,212	809,362
Gold Supplier members	18,682	27,384	43,028	96,110	121,274
International TrustPass	10,843	12,152	16,136	17,786	10,434
China TrustPass	189,573	266,009	372,876	501,316	67,765

[29] Alibaba.com, "Financial Reports": http://ir.alibaba.com/ir/home/financial_reports.htm.

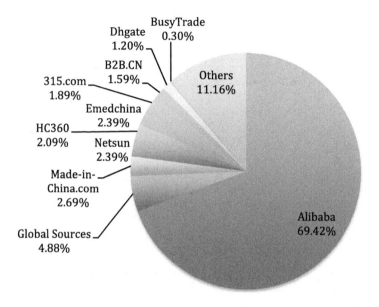

Exhibit 3.   Chinese online B2B companies' revenues in 2010, quarter 4.[30]

[30] iResearch Reports, "Q4 2010 Quarterly Report on China Ecommerce".

- International market[31]

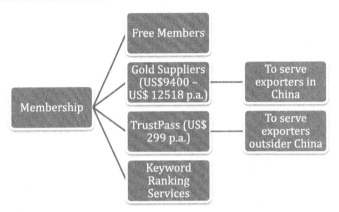

- Domestic market[32]

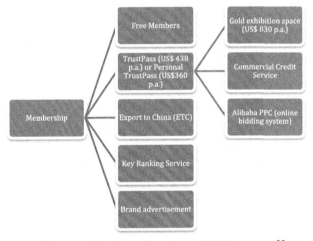

Exhibit 4. Product Overview of Alibaba.com[33]

---

[31] More information see: http://img.alibaba.com/others/popup/trust_030325.html

[32] More information about Export To China see: http://www.alibaba.com/activities/export_to_china/export_to_china_get_in.html

[33] http://service.alibaba.com/ggs/learning.htm

Li Ning: Make the Change

Jiawen Tu

LI NING — THE COMPANY

As one of China's leading sports goods companies, Li Ning has been growing rapidly these years. In 2011, Li Ning had a revenue of 8,928.5 million RMB with 98.1% in the domestic market and 1.9% in the international market.[1] In 2009, it achieved a net profit of 945 million RMB in the year, and for the first time the company overtook its major foreign competitor, Adidas. In the sports goods market, Li Ning is now the second biggest brand, only next to Nike.

The company was founded in 1990 by Mr. Li Ning, a former Chinese Olympic gymnast. Born in 1963, Mr. Li Ning started training at the age of eight and was selected to join the national team in 1980. During his international sports career, Mr. Li Ning won 106 gold medals and became a two-time World Cup Champion in gymnastics. In 1982, Mr. Li Ning won six of seven medals awarded at the Sixth World Cup Gymnastic Competition, earning him the title "Prince of gymnastics". He is most famous for winning six medals at the 1984 Summer Olympics, the first Summer Olympics that the People's Republic of China participated. Mr. Li Ning is a legend in Chinese sports.

---

[1] Lining.com, Financial Highlights, 2011 Annual Results. http://www.lining.com/eng/ir/finhigh.php.

After retiring from his athlete career, Mr. Li Ning joined Guangdong Jianlibao Group as a special assistant to the General Manager. He gained valuable business experience and handled a promotional campaign of Jianlibao sports drinks. Half a year later, Mr. Li Ning established a sports goods company containing his name — the "Guangdong Li Ning Sports Goods Company Limited" in 1990. In the same year the company won the bid to sponsor the Asian Games held in Beijing and Mr. Li Ning decided to name the company's products after himself as he felt that his fame would lend instant credibility to the product. And so the brand "Li Ning" was born. The company supplied 10,000 suits of "Li Ning" branded clothes to participants in the games.[2] The company was an instant success and was soon selling products throughout China. In 1992 Li Ning's products were chosen as the sportswear for the national team during the Olympic Games in Barcelona. It was also the first time that the Chinese team wore their own brands in the Olympic Games.

The foundation period was followed by one of high-speed development from 1995 to 1997, during which Li Ning became the dominant domestic sports brand. The Asian financial crisis in 1997 promoted a re-organization of Li Ning's strategy, organization structure, and personnel structure. The quality of the products was enhanced with the establishment of a development center and the introduction of international designers. In 1999, Li Ning installed SAP systems to automate functions like finance, human resources management, sales, and warehouse management. In 2001, sales of the company reached 734 million yuan. In 2002 Li Ning renewed its image by launching the slogan "Anything is Possible".

June 28, 2004, the company was listed on the Hong Kong Stock Exchange to raise its funds for its brand promotion efforts, retail chain expansion, product research and development. Li Ning intensified its efforts to achieve transparency and adopted a coherent vision and system values. Internationalization of the brand became a major part of the business strategy. In March 2006, Li Ning 001 Limited

---

[2] S. Tejomoortula and R. Fernando (2006) Li Ning: Brand Growth and Excellence in China, *ICMR Center for Management Research 506-049-1*, P4.

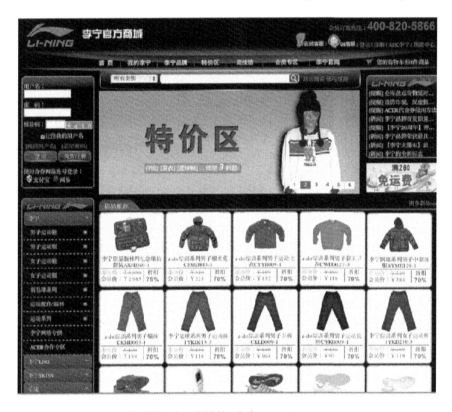

Exhibit 1. Li Ning's internet store

Edition shoes was launched. This was the first time ever a Chinese sports brand started selling a limited edition sneaker. In 2008, Li Ning cooperated with Taobao.com, a leading commercial website in China, and opened its special stores on the Internet (Refer to Exhibit I). In the summer of 2008, Mr. Li Ning was selected as the final torchbearer of the 29th Olympic games in Beijng, which not only was a special honor to the prince himself but also promoted the image of the company greatly as well.

LI NING'S SUCCESS FACTORS

Branding is the core competency of Li Ning. At the beginning of the foundation of the company, Li Ning understood clearly the importance of branding and was fully aware to establish a brand. In the 1990s, there were few companies or brands named by celebrities, thus it seemed to be quite wise to establish a sports goods company and name it after a sports celebrity. On one hand, since Mr. Li Ning has been very famous in China, the company became well known rapidly by using his name as a brand. On the other hand, Mr. Li Ning is not only famous but also has a good image. His effort for his sports career shows an upward and progressive spirit. Moreover, Mr. Li Ning is seen as a national hero for his perfect performances in competitions. All of these aspects added to the image of the company.

After the company was founded, it established a set of brand strategies to promote its products. By cooperating with Chinese national teams, Li Ning positioned its products as high-end products from the beginning. Li Ning sponsored the national teams in the 11th Asian Games in Beijing, the 25th Olympic Games in Barcelona, the 26th Olympic Games in Atlanta, the 27th Olympic Games in Sydney, and the 28th Olympic Games in Athens. Though Li Ning was not the official sponsor of the 29th Olympic Games in Beijing in 2008, in a market survey, 37.4% respondents thought Li Ning was the official sponsor (in contrast to 22.8% for the official sponsor Adidas).[3]

Li Ning has also sponsored all kinds of college-students sporting events, which helped the company to establish a good image. In 2002, a national college-student five-player football league competition named after Li Ning was held in Beijng, Tianjin, Shanghai and the 10 other provinces in China. In 2004, the company signed a four-year cooperation agreement with the Chinese University Basketball Association (CUBA) and it became the only sponsor of the association. Li Ning also cooperated with China University student Sports Association to help with promoting football in China.

As the first overseas store was launched in Santander, Spain in 2001, Li Ning began to promote its brand in the markets abroad. In 2002 the company sponsored the Spanish national team in the 14th World Women's Basketball Championships. In 2005, Li Ning signed with the American National Basketball Association (NBA) and

---

[3] Author unknown, *Li Ning vs. Adidas*, Tencent net. http://finance.qq.com/a/20080808/002357.htm [12 December 2010]

became its official partner. Cleveland Cavaliers' Damon Jones had been wearing Li Ning shoes since 2005, and in 2006 superstar Shaquille O'Neal signed a five-year deal with Li Ning. The company is also an official partner of the Association of Tennis Professionals (ATP) and had sponsored the national teams of other countries like Argentina, Vietnam and Sudan.

Furthermore, Li Ning has a high sense of social responsibility, which helps to promote the company's image. It donated 6 million RMB to the disaster provinces in the large flood in 1998. In 2008 the company donated 12.49 million RMB to the Wenchuan area, which suffered a big earthquake.

Li Ning's products portfolio contains apparel, footwear, and accessory products for sports and leisure. Li Ning's products are well perceived by customers. The quality of its products is on par with those of Nike and Adidas, yet the price of the products is much cheaper. In comparison of its domestic competitors, Li Ning's products are of a much better quality and more expensive than domestic competitors. Li Ning has a team of global design talents and two R&D centers. One is the Li Ning Sports Science Research and Development Center in Guangdong province, which specializes in sports science research, product testing, research and development of core technologies and enhancement of product functionalities. The other is the Global Innovation Center in Oregon, which specializes in the design, production, and testing of professional gears for Li-Ning-sponsored athletes and teams. Li Ning's major shoe lines include the "Flying Armor" series of basketball shoes and "Flying Feather" running shoes. Its hallmark product is the "Li-Ning bow" which was launched in 2006.

Li Ning's products are mainly sold through franchised distributions. There are three main kinds of retail stores: the department store, the stand-alone store and the e-commercial store. In 2009, Li Ning had 7,249 stores in 1,800 cities in China. Li Ning is pursuing a strategy of channel penetration that focuses on second- and third-tier cities where approximately 76% of its stores are located.[4] Although consumers in second- and third-tier cities have a substantially lower

---

[4] J. Meuer and L. DiVito, "A Grand Entrance? Li Ning's Emergence as a Global, Chinese Brand.", *RSM Case Development Center*, 2010, 310-138-1, p5.

income level and thus consumption, these markets show the highest growth potential and 80% of all new Li Ning stores are located in these markets.⁵ Li Ning has 11 flagship stores in prime locations in major first-tier cities. These flagship stores are intended to increase the influence of the Li Ning' brand and drive sales.

On July 1, 2010, Li Ning launched a new logo and announced its new brand slogan "Make the Change". The logo, which is similar to the previous brand invented by the founder of the company Mr. Li Ning, now includes a break line and is said to resemble the Chinese character "人" which means "people". It "conveys a tough, motion- and energy-rich silhouette", Mr. Li Ning said, "and it helps communicate the brand's sports values to a new generation".⁶ The updated slogan, which is also part of the company's new image, replaced the old company adage of "Anything Is Possible" and makes the company more distinctive than before. The old logo and the slogan strongly resembled the logo of their man international competitor Nike. The slogan "Anything is Possible" was also considered to be inspired by Nike's slogan "Nothing is impossible". This led to strong criticism in the sports industry. To find success the company must shake the suspicion that it copied its Western rival and become a more recognizable brand.

Anything is Possible   Make the Change

Previous Logo and Slogan   New Logo and Slogan

Despite of its great success, for years, Li Ning had been criticized for its previous logo and slogan, which bore a strong resemblance to the Nike "Swoosh" design and Adidas slogan "Impossible Is Nothing".

---

⁵ Ibid.

⁶ N. DePaula, Li-Ning Unveils New Logo & Brand Slogan, *SOLE ISSUE 36* http://solecollector.com/Sneakers/News/Li-Ning-Unveils-New-Logo-Brand-Slogan/ [12 December 2010]

In 2010, however, Li Ning changed, not only because it attempts to reach out to the new generation, but it needs a new image to compete with foreign competitors in the overseas market as well. "The Company felt we needed to become more refreshed, more energetic and unique, proactively inserting our Chinese history into a global audience," said Jay Li, General Manager of Li-Ning International. "This new logo will hopefully communicate both Li-Ning's continued evolution into sports culture and our continued pride in our heritage".[7]

As Jay Li said, Li Ning is trying to bring this Chinese brand to global consumers now. Since Li Ning has already succeeded in the domestic market, it began to expand its influence outside China. In fact, just no more than five months earlier before the company changed its logo and slogan, Li Ning opened a retail store in the United States (Portland, Oregon).[8] It is the first Li Ning store in the US and the move was seen as the milestone in the company's approach to being global. Since Nike's headquarter is also in Portland, it seems that Li Ning has begun to compete with Nike directly now. The company is fearless and confident. Li-Ning CEO Zhang Zhiyong says in regard to the goal of the company: "*By 2018, we expect the company to be one of the top five sports goods companies in the world*".[9]

MAKE THE CHANGE

The launch of a new logo and slogan was just in time for Li Ning. It gave Li Ning an opportunity to reposition itself in the market and helped the company to compete in the overseas market. Li Ning upgraded its logo and slogan, getting near to its goal of being a leader

---

[7] J. Brilliant, *Li-Ning Logo & Brand Revitalization*, CounterKicks.com http://CounterKicks.com/2010/07/02/li-ning-logo-brand-revitalization [12 December 2010]

[8] A. Brettman, *Li-Ning Makes a move into U.S. Running shoes market*, OregonLive.com, http://www.oregonlive.com/business/index.ssf/2010/10/li-ning_makes_a_move_into_us_r.html [12 December 2010]

[9] Author unknown, *Li Ning makes the change to catch up*, China.org.cn, http://www.china.org.cn/business/2010-07/01/content_20392314.htm [12 December 2010]

in the world. As the economy in China grows rapidly, consumers have more money and they become more and more interested in sports. After the 2008 Olympic Games, more and more people got interested in doing sports. The Chinese super sports stars like Yao Ming and Liu Xiang inspired people's interest in sports. The consumer market is still huge.

Facing sharp market competition, Li Ning took badminton as a breakthrough to compete with Nike of which basketball is the main field and Adidas of which football is the main field. Badminton is very popular in China and southeast Asia. And it is easier to standardize the equipment of these sports than basketball and football in the overseas market. In southeast Asia, Li Ning has opened approximately 100 badminton product spots. In 2009 Li Ning replaced Yonex as the main sponsor of the Chinese national team of badminton.[10]

Different from other commercial brands, a sports brand always has its own personality and value, which must be recognized and accepted by consumers. Li Ning has its own mission and value. As he says, "Through sports, we inspire people with the desire and power to make breakthroughs", Li Ning is just trying to do its best to let Chinese people be proud of their own products, as they once were proud of their sports champion. Furthermore, as an individual Li Ning needs sporting spirits like working hard and being courageous to achieve success in his own life. In this sense, Li Ning is far more than a sports brand.

TAKING A CHINESE BRAND UPSCALE

Chinese Consumers

Though Li Ning had achieved great success in the last two decades, as the former consumers of the 1990s reach middle-age, the Li Ning the brand seemed to be old to some extent. Between 2006 and 2007, Li Ning did a survey and found that over 50% of its consumers were

---

[10]Author unknown, *Thought on the change of Li Ning's logo*, job168.com (http://www.job168.com/info/read-80038.html) [12 December 2010]

35 to 40 years old, which was far from the company's target.[11] The best age of consumers for a sports goods company is from 14 to 25. However, most young consumers found, compared with international famous brands, Li Ning was not cool, factional and international. The CEO of Li Ning was aware of the problem and said, "Though Li Ning was regarded as the best brand in the over 25-year-old consumers, it was regarded not as good as Nike and Adidas".[12] Moreover, as Li Ning for years had focused on sales in the second- and third-tier cities, the brand did not appeal to young consumers in the market of first-tier cities where Nike and Adidas dominated. The company was at the risk of becoming a second-rate brand. If it wanted to maintain its position in the market, it had to reach out to the post-90s consumers.

Many Chinese consumers are unwilling to follow a Chinese brand upmarket. If their income rises they usually start buying more expensive foreign brand.[13] This benefits companies like Adidas and Nike, but leaves Li Ning with the question on how to position itself in the Chinese market.

One attempt is to focus on other markets than China. Li Ning's goal is to build an international brand and to regard Nike and Adidas as its main competitors. The company's vision is to be "a world's leading brand in the sports goods industry". As Mr. Li Ning said, "We do not want to be "Nike" from China; we want to be "Li Ning" in the world".[14] However, in 2009 the overseas sales only counted 1.1% which is much less than the domestic sales. Meantime, in the same year Li Ning beat Adidas in the domestic market and gained the second position, which was the best in the past five years. When the company opened its store in Oregon early in 2010, it showed it is ready for internationalization.

The new logo was part of this strategy. "The new logo was designed to appeal to young people who like changing, especially the post-90s

---

[11] Ibid.

[12] Ibid.

[13] P. Waldmeir, (2011) "Ning Raises concerns for Chinese brands." Financial Times.

[14] Z. Wang, *To be Li Ning in the world, not Nike from China*, 163.com, http://money.163.com/09/0910/20/5ISILFQJ00253JPP.html [8 January 2011]

consumers", Zhang Zhi Yong, an executive Director of Li Ning, said.[15] The new logo which maintained part of the previous one shows the shape of the Chinese character "人", which means that everybody can can express their good qualities and realize their potentials through sports. And the previous slogan "Anything is Possible" might have encouraged people to think, but the new slogan "Make the Change" encourages people to do. During these 20 years, from "Anything is Possible" to "Make the Change", the Li-Ning brand has weathered challenges from the market well and has evolved from an infant into an energetic young man fond of taking challenges. "Today, the changes for the Li-Ning brand go well beyond a change of logo. The Li-Ning brand needs to pursue a better-defined strategic positioning, more innovative ways of thinking, operating systems that highlight the features of sports brand management, and professional capabilities that are more competitive. The step we take today is a determined one that will take us to becoming a world-class brand as we integrate our resources in brand management, sports marketing, product designs, technological innovations and human resources onto a global platform", Mr. Li Ning said at the 20th anniversary of the company.[16]

THE FUTURE OF LI NING

Li Ning's main competitors Nike and Adidas have dominated the market in the first-tier cities for nearly six years and they might further compete with domestic enterprises in the second- and third-tier cities. If Li Ning wants to compete with its international competitors it must penetrate the first-tier cities and attract the attention of the young generation. Meanwhile the company has to keep its position in the second- and third-tier cities. Besides the international competitors, Li Ning also faces competition from domestic companies like Anta,

---

[15] Author unknown, *Thought on the change of Li Ning's logo*, job168.com, http://www.job168.com/info/read-80038.html [12 December 2010]

[16] Press Release, *The Li-Ning Brand Celebrated its 20th Anniversary Taking a Bold Step to Becoming a World-class Brand*, Li Ning Company Limited website, http://www.lining.com/EN/press/inside-3_1_53.html [12 December 2010]

Peak, Hongxing Erke which are very successful in China as well and exerts great pressure on Li Ning in the second- and third-tier cities.

In the overseas market where Nike and Adidas have advantages there are just a few Li Ning stores. The foreign customers may know the brand but they may never have tried Li Ning products. If Li Ning wants to compete with international brands in the overseas market it needs to expand its stores and influence.

Being international players is the dream of all Chinese enterprises, but it is not easy. There are still few Chinese companies that are successful in the overseas market. However, they never stop. When the chairman of board of Lenovo heard that Li Ning was upgrading its brand, he reminded that Lenovo had done the same before the company went to the overseas market. He said, "I am happy that Li Ning is going to the international market, because we need more Chinese brands, only one or two companies are not enough. I hope Li Ning is aware that the way to the overseas market is very hard but the market is also huge".[17] It is true that Chinese brands are not well known in the world now. Most foreigners' impression of "Made in China" is it is cheap. It is to be seen, whether Li Ning will be successful in internationalizing its brand. Time is pressing. Li Ning's profit has fallen 57% since the beginning of 2011.

So far Li Ning has grown the company by copying Western rivals, focusing on the Chinese market. It is time to change and grow into an international brand recognized in China and overseas. But how can this be done? Will Li Ning's new image be able to gain recognition of the new generation and consumers overseas? Will Li Ning succeed in the global market and become the next Nike in the future?

BIBLIOGRAPHY

A. Brettman, Li-Ning Makes a move into U.S. Running shoes market, OregonLive. com, http://www.oregonlive.com/business/index.ssf/2010/10/li-ning_makes_a_move_into_us_r.html [12 December 2010]

---

[17] Author unknown, *Thought on the change of Li Ning's logo*, job168.com, http://www.job168.com/info/read-80038.html [12 December 2010]

Author unknown, Li Ning makes the change to catch up, China.org.cn, http://www.china.org.cn/business/2010-07/01/content_20392314. htm [12 December 2010]

Author unknown, Li Ning vs. Adidas, Tencent net, http://finance.qq. com/a/20080808/002357.htm [12 December 2010]

Author unknown, Thought on the change of Li Ning's logo, job168.com, http://www.job168.com/info/read-80038.html [12 December 2010]

J. Brilliant, Li-Ning Logo & Brand Revitalization, CounterKicks.com, http:// CounterKicks.com/2010/07/02/li-ning-logo-brand-revitalization/ [12 December 2010]

J. Meuer and L. DiVito, "A Grand Entrance? Li Ning's Emergence as a Global, Chinese Brand.", RSM Case Development Center, 2010, 310-138-1, p5.

L. Watheu, G. Wang and M. Samant, Li Ning-Anything is Possible, Harvard Business School, REV March 19, 2007, 9-507-024

N. DePaula, Li-Ning Unveils New Logo & Brand Slogan, SOLE ISSUE 36, http://solecollector.com/Sneakers/News/Li-Ning-Unveils-New-Logo-Brand-Slogan/ [12 December 2010]

Press Release, The Li-Ning Brand Celebrated its 20th Anniversary Taking a Bold Step to Becoming a World-class Brand, Li Ning Company Limited website, http://www.lining.com/EN/press/inside-3_1_53.html [12 December 2010]

Lining.com, Financial Highlights, 2011 Annual Result. http://www.lining. com/eng/ir/finhigh.php

P. Waldmeir, 2011, Ning Raises concerns for Chinese brands, Financial Times

S. Tejomoortula and R. Fernando, 2006, Li Ning: Brand Growth and Excellence in China, ICMR Center for Management Research 506-049-1, P4.

Z. Wang, To be Li Ning in the world, not Nike from China, 163.com, http:// money.163.com/09/0910/20/5ISILFQJ00253JPP.html [8 January 2011]

http://www.lining.com/EN/company/inside-1_1.html

http://en.wikipedia.org/wiki/Li_Ning_(company)

http://www.e-lining.com/

http://baike.baidu.com/view/10670.htm

Shiseido in China — When Politics Interferes with Business

Kaoutar Lazrak

THE COMPANY

Shiseido Company Limited is the leading cosmetics company in Japan — and indeed a world leader — as well as one of the oldest. At the end of March 2012, the company's capital was 64.5 billion yen and the consolidated net sales were 682.4 billion yen. The company's 46,267 employees make great efforts to accomplish Shiseido's mission to "create beauty and wellness," and do so in 87 different countries.[1]

In 1872, only four years after the Meiji Restoration, Arinobu Fukuhara, a former chief pharmacist at a navy hospital, founded the first Western-style pharmacy in Japan, in Ginza, the most exclusive area of Tokyo. He chose a name that would be associated with luxury and the exclusive location. Shiseido (資生堂) can be translated as "praising the virtues of the earth which nurtures new life and brings forth significant values".

The company prospered, and in 1915 Shinzo Fukuhara (the founder's son) transformed Shiseido's pharmacy business into a cosmetics brand, combining research, development and high-quality manufacturing. Shiseido became the first cosmetics company in the

---

[1] Shiseido group's official website, http://group.shiseido.com/company/. [23 January 2013].

world. A year later, Shinzo Fukuhara, now the company's first president, established a research and development laboratory which demonstrated a level of innovation and quality that was unique at the time.[2]

Despite the difficulties that the company faced at the beginning of the 20th century, Shiseido came up with very innovative ideas. World War I and the Great Kanto Earthquake did not help the cosmetics industry, and relations with retailers were particularly suffering due to a price war between cosmetics competitors. It was in this context that the company introduced the Shiseido Cosmetics Chain Store System in 1923, with the objective of improving its relations with stores, where "it profitably sold its toothpaste, perfumes, facial powders, vanishing creams and soaps".[3] The system was based on a contractual partnership between Shiseido and its distributors, who would themselves agree on a contract with their retailers. The contract was a way to specify a set price common to all retailers selling Shiseido products.[4] This system, invented by Shiseido in 1923, is still the most popular in the cosmetics industry today.

The Camellia Club, a service for loyal Shiseido customers, was founded in 1937. To coincide with the formation of the club, Shiseido issued a fashion periodical, HANATSUBAKI (Camellia). The magazine was Japan's first cultural magazine by a cosmetics company, and was issued by Shiseido from 1924 for distribution to customers through the nationwide network of stores. Originally named SHISEIDO GRAPH in 1933, it became HANATSUBAKI in 1937, when the club was founded. HANATSUBAKI magazine offered articles on domestic and overseas fashion, travel, and the arts. Essays and commentaries by leading literary figures of the time were also fea-

---

[2] Shiseido's history, http://group.shiseido.com/company/past/history/. [23 January 2013].

[3] E. Corkill (2010) "Mr Shiseido' blends beauty and business", *Japan Times*, March 7, 2010. http://www.japantimes.co.jp/text/fl20100307x1.html. [23 January 2013].

[4] Shiseido Asia Official Website, http://www.asia.shiseido.com/about/story/origins/16.htm. [23 January 2013].

tured in the magazine, which is still issued on a monthly basis by Shiseido today. The Camellia Club now boasts a membership of approximately 9 million members (see History and Background of Shiseido).[5]

The year 1941 marked the beginning of the company's expansion beyond cosmetics. That year, Shiseido began managing restaurants and selling confectionery. Thus, Shiseido Food Sales Co., Ltd. was created (now Shiseido Parlour Co., Ltd.). Continuing its expansion towards new industries, the group launched Shiseido Pharmaceutical Co., Ltd. in 1987, and started to sell health food and pharmaceuticals.

In 1986, the group also began to sell non-Shiseido brands in order to diversify the company's products and reach different customers. The make-up products of IPSA were the first non-Shiseido brand marketed by the group. The same year saw many foreign acquisitions by the group, with the aim of enriching the company's portfolio with prestigious brands such as Carita in France.

Another important year for Shiseido was 1991, when the first production facility opened in Europe, following the existing ones in North America and Taiwan. This demonstrates the global production network the group has progressively built worldwide.

Shiseido has a strong corporate policy based on a few main features. Firstly, Shiseido is committed to answering the needs of its customers thanks to high product quality and regular technological innovations. Secondly, the company is successful thanks to the broad geographical area in which Shiseido's products are both produced and distributed. Figure 1 presents an overview of the business areas in which the company is active.

The Company's Strategy

Shiseido Group has always been committed to its customers, making the world of beauty and wellness more accessible to them. One of the

---

[5] History and Background of Shiseido. http://www.fragrancex.com/products/_bid Shiseido-am-cid_skincare-am-lid_S_brand_history.html [23 January 2013]

Domestic Cosmetics Business: Products & Services for the Japanese Market

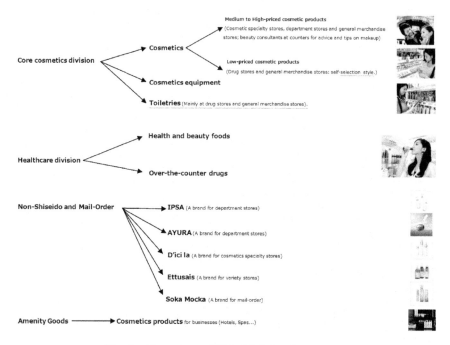

Fig. 1   Overview of Shiseido's business areas.

keys to Shiseido's success is its technological advances, which allow the brand to create innovative products that reach the more demanding customer's needs. The first factor that led Shiseido to this position was its original alliance of Japanese and Western ingredients. The fusion of Eastern theory and Western science has been a very intelligent compromise that, since its creation, has helped the cosmetic brand gain an important competitive advantage.

In Asian hygiene and beauty culture, plants have always been very important. That's why Shiseido continues to use natural Japanese ingredients that make its products unique. One of these ingredients is rice bran, which is rich in minerals and fibre; it is used for polishing and exfoliating of excess skin cells. Another Japanese ingredient is camellia oil, which is used for hair treatments. Mukuroji extract (or Soap berry in English), which is obtained from a tree found in Japan, has a powerful effect that helps prevent wrinkles. Finally, we should mention Uji green tea, which is the highest quality Japanese green tea found in the southern region of Kyoto. Its extract helps provide potent antioxidant effects and prevent cellular damage caused by UV rays.[6]

Shiseido is unique not only because of its ingredients, but also because of its important investments in research and development. The brand has revolutionized the cosmetics industry thanks to its innovative skin measurement technologies, among other things. Shiseido collaborates with scientists at research institutes and universities worldwide, such as the MGH/Harvard Cutaneous Biology Research Center. It has more than 2,300 international patents, proving its innovative technologies. Finally, the technology awards gained by the company show its cutting-edge findings, as described in Shiseido's 2012 annual report: "The Company's record of top technology awards demonstrates its world-leading position in cosmetics research and development." Shiseido has won 15 top awards from the International Federation of Societies of Cosmetic Chemists (IESCC) conferences and congresses, positioning Shiseido Group as the cosmetics company which achieves the highest number of top technological awards.

Moreover, thanks to the approximately 1,000 researchers at the Global Technology Sites which Shiseido has established worldwide, the company can research and develop products adapted to each significant market, using local products to be closer to each customer and building a strong relationship based on trust with the customers of each market. In fact, Shiseido has Research & Development centers in every important market where the company is present.[7] The presence of these technological centers allows the company to

---

[6] http://group.shiseido.com/rd/about/unique.html. The company's official website. [24 May 2013]
[7] For more details see Appendix 1.

research the local market and to provide local products and conduct marketing studies among customers in each area.

SHISEIDO, A GLOBAL BRAND

Shinzo Fukuhara, the company's first president, studied Eastern medicine in Japan, before graduating from Columbia University's Faculty of Medicine. During his stay in the United States, from 1908, he worked at a suburban New York drug store and later the cosmetics factory of an American pharmaceutical manufacturer.

But it was Mr. Fukuhara's first encounter with Paris which determined the identity of the brand, clearly influencing the aesthetic of Shiseido. As the founder of Shiseido as a cosmetic brand, Mr. Fukuhara reflects the brand's identity, which explains why the company entered markets beyond the limited domestic one so early. Under his leadership, the groundwork for a distinctive Shiseido approach to business was formed.[8] Yoshiharu Fukuhara, Shinzo's nephew, confirmed in an interview for the *Japan Times*: "The notion that Shiseido had to look abroad was set out by my uncle Shinzo and his friend Noboru Matsumoto [who served as the second president]. Both had studied in the United States, so both had very international perspectives".[9]

The year 1957 marks a turning point in the internationalization of the brand, when Shiseido launched its first overseas operations among Taiwan's Japanese community. The group continued its expansion in Hawaii in 1962, followed by the United States three years later, while the first European country penetrated was Italy in 1963. The company launched its first stores in China in 1981, and started its operations in Russia in 1999.[10] An important point to note is that the company exported not only stores but also production

---

[8] History and Background of Shiseido, 2013, *op cit.*
[9] E. Corkill (2010). "Mr. Shiseido' blends beauty and business," *Japan Times*, March 7, 2010; Interview with Yoshiharu Fukuhara, grandson of Shiseido's founder: http://www.japantimes.co.jp/text/fl20100307×2.html. [23 January 2013]
[10] *Ibid.*

facilities to North America, Taiwan, and Europe. In 1993 the company opened its first Chinese factory in Beijing, as we will see later. In 2010, a factory also opened in Vietnam. It has thus established a global production network that has enabled Shiseido's success all over the world.

When entering a new foreign market, the group has used a strategy based on three main points to help in its success: to emphasize the company's originality, to use local resources as much as possible, and to establish roots in the local community as a good corporate citizen.[11]

SHISEIDO, A DIVERSIFIED AND MULTI-BRAND COMPANY[12]

Shiseido is a diversified company, covering different industries and not only offering cosmetics. But the group also stocks many different brands, targeting different customers. Some of these brands have been developed by the group, and others have been gained through acquisitions. What characterizes all the brands sold by Shiseido is a strong brand image.

The five main areas of Shiseido's development are the **Cosmetics Business** (cosmetics, cosmetics equipment, and toiletries); the **Professional Division** (hair and beauty products for hair salons); the **Healthcare Division** (health and beauty foods and over-the-counter drugs); the **Frontier Sciences Division** (cosmetic raw materials, medical-use drugs, beauty care cosmetics); and the **Food Business** (restaurant L'Osier, sales of confectionery, wines, and imported foods).[13]

---

[11] Interview with Rika Takahashi, Director, Global Planning Office, Technical Division, SHISEIDO Co., LTD., reported in the Institute for International Studies and Training's website: http://www.iist.or.jp/wf/magazine/0762/0762_E.html. [23 January 2013]

[12] See Appendix 2.

[13] Shiseido business webpage, http://group.shiseido.com/company/business/group.html [23 January 2013]

From 1986, Shiseido decided to expand the brand portfolio both by acquisitions and by creating new brands, such as those mentioned above. Some examples of the important acquisitions made by the group are bareMinerals, NARS, Jean Paul Gaultier, and Issey Miyake.

SHISEIDO IN CHINA

Shiseido's brand name is derived from the classic Chinese text the *Yi Jing*.[14] This expression, as translated above, is directly in line with Shiseido's mission to serve people and contribute to the world through beauty and wellness. However, although the brand's name was inspired by Chinese culture 140 years ago, this does not mean that China has been part of Shiseido's history from the start. Because of the unstable political and economic situation in China before the 1980s, Shiseido had to wait until 1981 to enter the Chinese market, when the nation had just begun to open its economy to foreign companies.

Shiseido entered the Chinese market 24 years after the company started to internationalize. It was following a request from the city of Beijing that the company turned towards China. To begin with, Shiseido only imported and sold around 60 items through hotels and retail stores in Beijing.[15] But at that time, the culture of purchasing fashionable and cosmetic products was not yet imbedded in Chinese people's minds. Most of Shiseido's customers were foreigners living in Beijing. Then came the first (of four) Technological Cooperation Agreement between the city of Beijing and Shiseido, which was aimed at changing this. In 1983, the company shared production technology with a daily commodity factory in Beijing, in line with the agreement. This cooperation with a local factory enabled Shiseido to distinguish itself from the other foreign companies operating in China

---

[14] Institute for International Studies and Training World Forum: http://www.iist. or.jp/wf/magazine/0762/0762_E.html [23 January 2013]

[15] Press Release published by Shiseido Group on 2011/9/14: Shiseido's Global Vision: China at the Helm of Broad-based Expansion Strategy. http://group. shiseido.com/releimg/1931-e.pdf [23 January 2013]

(mainly European and American brands) and to develop a strong long-term relationship with Chinese customers. Thanks to this cooperation Shiseido developed new shampoos, hair-styling products, cosmetics, and skin-care products.

The success of this alliance led Shiseido and the city of Beijing to deepen their relationship in 1991 by creating a joint venture company, the Shiseido Liyuan Cosmetics Co., Ltd. The objective was to develop, produce, and sell new prestigious cosmetic products, specifically tailored to the Chinese clientele. Two years later, the factory built exclusively for Shiseido Liyuan Cosmetics was ready, and the AUPRES brand was launched in 1994. AUPRES was a brand created exclusively for the Chinese market and is still one of Shiseido's most important brands in China. Its name means "close to" in French, a reference to Shiseido's aim to be as close as possible to its customers. Indeed, the brand was researched, created, and produced in China, within the new factory of Shiseido Liyuan Cosmetics. One example of AUPRES's success, and its recognition as a "national" brand, was its selection as the official cosmetics brand for the Chinese athletes participating in the Sydney Olympics in 2000 and the Athens Olympics in 2004.

The group continued to expand the local development and production of Chinese products using the same strategy. The company completed the construction of another factory in Shanghai in 1998, as the city's growth could no longer be ignored. The company opened its first Shiseido China Research Center in Beijing in 2001, in order to promote research into traditional Chinese herbal medicine.[16] Unlike Western cosmetics brands present in China, Shiseido uses the Chinese culture that Chinese people know and trust.

The year 2003 was also an important milestone, as it was in this year that Shiseido decided to establish its subsidiary Shiseido China Co., Ltd. in Shanghai, and two years later the Sales and Marketing department was transferred to China as well. In 2006, the company developed URARA, an exclusive brand for cosmetics specialty stores, in line with its brand image associated with "prestige", "high quality", and "safety".

---

[16] *Ibid.*

It seems relevant to underline the opening of a Training Center in China in 2008, as it demonstrates the importance of the educational aspect of Shiseido's strategy in China. Rika Takahashi, Director of the Global Planning Office in the Technical Division of the company, confirms this point in an interview given to the Institute for International Studies and Training: "We put a lot of time and effort into personnel development, and since setting up our training center in Shanghai in 2008, we have been providing education there for company employees, sales staff, and employees in the chain stores of companies selling our products".[17] This is another point that clearly differentiates Shiseido from its competitors. The cosmetics culture in China is young and people need to be reassured about their choices. Patricia Pao, CEO of the Pao Principle, a global consulting firm based in New York, explains in an article published in AdAge China that "beauty is still relatively new to Chinese women, so education is a valuable tool for consumers — and an opportunity for marketers. Mao Zedong forbid the use of cosmetics until the 1980s, so beauty information was virtually non-existent until then. While today's Western woman is generally initiated into the beauty ritual by her mom, Chinese women are dependent on outside sources for their beauty information".[18]

In 2010, Shiseido's aim to be accessible to every potential customer and in all areas led the company to launch the brand DQ, commercialized in drugstores. The company's choice to develop into this new channel is directly in line with its customer target. Women who look for cosmetics products in drugstores are aware of skin troubles and expect products from the drugstore to be at the forefront of technology. Shiseido has responded to the expectations of this clientele, emphasizing that it has kept its focus on research and development ever since the company was founded.

---

[17] *Ibid.*

[18] Article written by Patricia Pao published in AdAgeChina on September 01, 2010, http://adage.com/china/article/viewpoint/why-shiseido-beats-western-beauty-marketers-in-china/145645/. [23 January 2013]

It should be noted that Chinese customers place greater significance on the technological aspect of cosmetics products, due to the difference in their skin type. "The definition of beauty has become homogenized by the globalization of media, but there are cultural and societal differences that affect the way women in different countries view and use beauty products, especially in China".[19] Shiseido has understood this difference and has focused its research and development on this particular point. That is why Shiseido's knowledge of Chinese customers, which is better than those Western competitors who often do not adapt their products to Asian skin, is a real competitive advantage. Indeed, according to Rika Takahashi, "[...] while people talk about 'Asians' as a homogenous group, Asian skin varies widely. A detailed knowledge of Asian skin is one of Shiseido's strengths, and we consider ourselves to be the Asian skin experts".[20]

In 2010, Shiseido began to promote full-scale development of professional haircare products for hair salons. The distributed brands were SHISEIDO PROFESSIONAL, which was already sold in Japan, Asia, and Oceania, and JOICO, which was marketed in the United States. Once again, the key to Shiseido's success in the professional haircare market is its knowledge, and more than a century of research into Asian customers and their black hair.

The company also provides training sessions to educate stylists about the brand's discoveries. It was with this aim that Shiseido developed "Shiseido Beauty Studios" in Shanghai and Beijing in 2009 (Fig. 2).

This unique training program for educating stylists on hair theories and the spirit of hospitality (referred to as *Omotenashi*, one of Shiseido's main principles) is held in the company's own beauty studios.

Finally, to pursue its aim to be present in all distribution channels with products adapted for each, the group has started its conquest of the Internet. In 2011, Shiseido launched an online business where Chinese customers could purchase a line of products exclusive to this

---

[19] *Ibid.*
[20] *Ibid.*

Fig. 2　Shiseido beauty studio in Shanghai.

channel. Shiseido's strategy in China is based on its progressive development within different channels: from importing Japanese items and selling them in hotels and retail stores, the company launched an exclusive brand for cosmetics specialty stores (URARA) and later developed an exclusive brand for drugstores (DQ) as well as professional haircare products for hair salons in the same year. And the latest channel to be developed is the Internet, where the objective is to target different customers, as profiles differ according to the channel, and to reach as many consumers as possible.[21,22] Moreover, Shiseido has focused its development in China on researching local needs and tastes, in order to develop brands exclusively for Chinese people (See Table 1). Shiseido has also taken into account China's cultural background, implementing different educational tools in order to make Chinese customers trust and choose the brand.

---

[21] *Ibid.*
[22] Shiseido's distribution channel strategy can be seen in Appendix 3.

Table 1. Shiseido's main sales channels in China (in 2009).[23]

Target	Channel	Business Overview and Product Lines
Prestige	Upscale department stores	Global brand *SHISEIDO* sold worldwide, *Clé de Peau BEAUTÉ*, locally manufactured prestige cosmetics **SUPREME AUPRES** and **AUPRES** are sold at individual sales counters.
Cosmetic specialty stores	Shiseido cosmetic specialty stores (chain store contract stores)	Cosmetics specialty stores that are developed by forming a contract with each privately managed cosmetic store by utilizing Shiseido's know-how accumulated in Japan. Sells products that are not handled in department stores and stores have expanded to approximately 4,300 as of September 2009. **URARA** brand, **PURE&MILD**, **UNO**, *Elixir Superieur*, *MELANOREDUCE (HAKU)*, *TSUBAKI*, etc.
Middle mass	Department stores	Sell **Za**, **AquaLabel**, **PURE&MILD**, **UNO** and other brands at separate sales counters from prestige cosmetics products.
	General merchandising stores, supermarkets and convenience stores	**Za**, **UNO**, **AQUAIR**, *TSUBAKI*, etc.
	General merchandising and cosmetic specialty stores *via* wholesalers	**Za**, **PURE&MILD**, etc.

Note: Brands indicated in **bold** are locally manufactured products.

---

[23] Press Release published on December 17, 2009, "Shiseido to Launch New DQ Brand for Drugstores in China."

The company has been extremely successful in China. Shiseido's China sales were $616 million in 2007, and in 2008 its Asia-Pacific sales (primarily China and excluding Japan) amounted to $1.02 billion.[24] "China's cosmetics market is currently valued at 1.7 trillion yen on a sales basis, and the number of people using cosmetics in China as of 2010 was about 100 million, exceeding the number in Japan".[25] That number is forecasted to grow to 200 million by 2015 and 400 million by 2020.[26] That is proof that the group has anticipated the potential of the Chinese market and, according to the figures, Shiseido's predictions for the growth of the Chinese cosmetics market were right (See Fig. 3, Annual Report 2012, Shiseido Group p. 47).

According to a study conducted in 2010 by Pao Principle, which interviewed 1,014 Chinese women mostly aged 20–29 who use beauty products, "Shiseido was the most-used skin-care brand by [...] panelists, due to the fact that Chinese believe that Japanese technology is the most cutting-edge. They also believe that Japanese skin is close to theirs and that Shiseido has the best understanding of their skincare needs".[27]

Masashi Kamata, director and president of Shiseido China in 2010, reported to the Shanghai Daily that "China, the most important market for Shiseido globally, is the main driver of the company's growth with its large base of consumers and rising awareness of skincare".[28] At this point, there can be no further doubts about the importance of the Chinese market for the Shiseido Group.

---

[24] Survey by McKinsey Company: [PDF] "Winning the Chinese Consumer," http://csi.mckinsey.com/Knowledge_by_region/Asia/China/Winning_the_Chinese_consumer.aspx. [23 January 2013].

[25] The Annual Report 2012 of Shiseido Group, http://group.shiseido.com/ir/library/annual/pdf/2012/anu00001.pdf [23 January 2013], page 46.

[26] Institute for International Studies and Training World Forum: http://www.iist.or.jp/wf/magazine/0762/0762_E.html [23 January 2013].

[27] *Ibid.*

[28] Article written by Pan Xiaoyi, "China puts shine on Shiseido", *Shanghai Daily*, February 23, 2010: http://www.shanghaidaily.com/article/print.asp?id=429210 [23 January 2013].

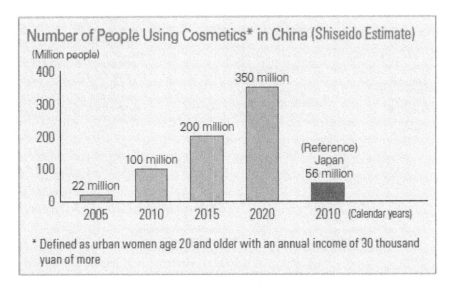

Fig. 3 Number of people using cosmetics in China, Shiseido annual report 2012.[29]

In 2011, Shiseido still had big hopes for its Chinese market, as reported in the *China Economic Review*, and the results demonstrate how much China influences the group's success: "Japan's biggest cosmetics maker, Shiseido [...] aims to increase its China sales by at least 15% per year as consumer incomes continue to rise, Bloomberg reported. China accounted for about 10% of Shiseido's [...] revenue in the fiscal year that ended in March 2010".[30]

Finally, the 2012 annual report confirms that the Chinese market is particularly important for the group's results: "Sales of our China business grew at a higher rate than the market as a whole".[31] The Chinese market is becoming increasingly vital for Shiseido, as it has been for many other Japanese firms.

---

[29] Annual Report 2012 of Shiseido Group, page 47.
[30] "Shiseido seeks to raise China sales by 15% a year," *China Economic Review*, January 21, 2011, http://www.chinaeconomicreview.com/node/51186 [23 January 2013]
[31] Annual report 2012, p. 44.

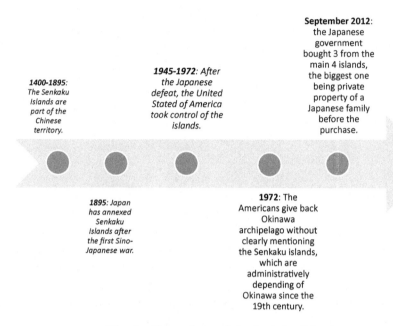

Fig. 4 Chronology of the Senkaku Islands.

However, relations between China and Japan have been complex for centuries. Shiseido has had to learn the hard way that politics and history have a much stronger influence on sales than the company could ever imagine.

CHINA–JAPAN POLITICAL CONTEXT

To begin with, it is important to understand that the political problem we are describing here has directly affected many Japanese companies that settled in China, and Shiseido is one of them. For an overview on this important factor contributing to Shiseido's success (or lack thereof) in China, let us consider this very brief chronology of the Senkaku Islands (See Fig. 4).[32]

---

[32] The chronology draws on information retracing the history of the islands, published in *Libération*, September 28, 2012: http://www.liberation.fr/monde/2012/09/28/japon-chine-pourquoi-la-guerre-des-iles_849311. [23 January 2013].

After the Japanese nationalization of the Senkaku Islands in September 2012, the Chinese reacted immediately, first with Prime Minister Wen Jiabao's declaration on 10th September that "The government and people of China will never budge even half an inch over the sovereignty and territorial issue".[33] Not only was there a political reaction to the Japanese move, but the Chinese population also turned aggressively against all things related to Japan (companies, stores, cars), putting in danger not only Japanese brands' customers, but also Japanese companies, and therefore the Japanese economy, which is obviously dependent on China, its main economic partner. The spontaneous reaction of the Chinese population was to boycott Japanese goods, including famous brands such as Suntory (drinks), Toyota (cars), Sony (electronics), and Shiseido. The boycott has been taken very seriously. Indeed, in a survey held following the dispute over the Senkaku Islands, to which 34,000 Chinese people responded, "40.6% of respondents said resolutely that they would not use Japanese goods again".[34] The protesters have also organized riots in many cities in China, demonstrating their animosity towards Japan. Among the slogans seen in these protests, one of the most succinct is: "Japan, get the hell out of China".[35]

It is important to understand that relation between China and Japan is very complex and have a significant impact on their respective economies, as the riots in China have demonstrated. We should note that the conflict between the Japanese and the Chinese populations is increasing in response to each event that provokes political

---

[33] "Senkakus standoff escalates as Chinese patrol boats approach", *The Asahi Shimbun*, September 11, 2012, http://ajw.asahi.com/article/special/isles_dispute/AJ201209110104 [23 January 2013].

[34] "As Islands Dispute Simmers, Survey Asks Chinese What They Like About Japan", *Worldcrunch*, 7 October 2012, http://worldcrunch.com/world-affairs/as-islands-dispute-simmers-survey-asks-chinese-what-they-like-about-japan/senkaku-diaoyu-japan-protests-/c1s9774/#.UP6R5ieG5Lc [23 January 2013].

[35] "Anti-Japan protests turn violent in Shenzhen, Guangzhou and Qingdao", *South China Morning Post*, 17 September 2012. http://www.scmp.com/news/china/article/1038664/anti-japan-protests-turn-violent-shenzhen-guangzhou-and-qingdao [23 January 2013].

tensions, such as the Senkaku Islands issue. Statistics show that "80% of citizens 'don't feel an affinity with China'".[36]

Now that we have seen how much the latest political crisis has affected both populations and economies, let us look at the figures which demonstrate what happened to Shiseido after the riots and boycotts.

In an article published in the *Wall Street Journal* on November 1, 2012, Hisayuki Suekawa, Shiseido's president, was reported to have declared: "Shiseido Co. (4911.TO), Japan's largest cosmetics maker, lowered its overseas revenue forecast for the year by 6 billion yen, of which 4–5 billion yen was attributable to China. Shiseido said sales in China dropped over 10% in September when the anti-Japan demonstrations took place. Even though it expects a pickup, 'Looking forward, we are not optimistic (about sales in China)".[37]

QUESTIONS

1. What are the factors contributing to Shiseido's success worldwide?
2. What are Shiseido's success factors in China?
3. How should Shiseido react to this crisis?
4. How can the company prevent a similar crisis in the future?

---

[36] Polly (2012) "Japanese Feel No Affinity With China and Korea, Shows Survey", *japanCRUSH*, 26 November, http://www.japancrush.com/2012/stories/japanese-feel-no-affinity-with-china-and-korea-shows-survey.html [23 January 2013].

[37] "Japan Firms See Billions of Dollars in Revenue Lost as Tokyo-Beijing Row Churns On", *The Wall Street Journal*, November 1, 2012, http://online.wsj.com/article/BT-CO-20121101-707323.html [23 January 2013].

Section II

JAPAN

UNIQLO: A Stitch in Time

Beatrice Reboux

BRAND NEW

The story of Uniqlo began in 1949, when Hitoshi Yanai founded Ogori Shoji, a men's clothing company, in Japan's Yamaguchi Prefecture, Ube. The main source of turnover was high-quality gentlemen's formal-wear. The company sourced its materials from Gifu and Nagoya, cities immersed in the textile industry. Yanai's son, Tadashi, graduated from Waseda University in 1971, went to work for JASCO, a large Japanese chain store, and finally joined his father's company in 1972. Alongside men's suits, Ogori Shoji sold high-quality women's dresses from foreign brands, and famous Japanese casual-wear brands such as VAN. In 1984, after Tadashi Yanai became the managing director, the small company extended its influence and opened the first Uniqlo shop in Hiroshima in 1985, under the name "Unique Clothing Warehouse." The name Uniqlo was later formed by fusing the first two words.

As the CEO, Tadashi Yanai had a clear, ambitious vision. Reminiscent of Steve Jobs, he is a man who has profound self-confidence and relentless drive, a style that contrasts sharply with the conformity often associated with Japanese culture.

From 1985, the so-called Japanese bubble economy marked high economic growth. As a result, expensive designers and brands became very popular in Japan. Tadashi Yanai, however, had other ideas, and began Uniqlo with the concept of selling casual wear at low prices. Even though Japan at the time was an expensive country, he was able to lower prices to the company's advantage for a number of reasons: 1) the mass procurement of private label products from overseas; 2) the opening of standardized stores in cost-saving locations; 3) a high degree of centralization of store management through the use of detailed manuals; and 4) narrow collections that still appealed to the needs of a broad range of consumers.

At this time, the Uniqlo concept that we know today was not yet fully developed. The shop inventory did not contain the Uniqlo brand. But the idea was well-established, as low prices featured in the stores and the "help-yourself" system was adopted. In contrast to luxury stores, where customers were meticulously served, the new concept meant that customers of casual wear could help themselves. Most of the Uniqlo inventory was imported. In 1985, Japan experienced a dramatic rise in the exchange rate of the yen. Nevertheless, the cost of the goods that Ogori Shoji needed stayed constant. Therefore, to achieve low prices at the point of sale, the company needed to reduce its overhead costs.

In 1985, Uniqlo opened in a suburb of Shimonoseki. At the end of the same year, two more Uniqlo shops opened in Okayama. The shops were built to look like warehouses to save on construction costs. This was one way of reducing overall costs.

Nevertheless, the opening of new stores made it difficult to find steady sources for products of good quality at low prices. To find cheaper suppliers, in 1987 Yanai went to Hong Kong and visited a company named Jelldarno, which sold a clothing brand of the same name. The brand was sold in the United States and Europe, and had a reputation for good quality and low cost. Yanai decided to commission the factory that manufactured the Jelldarno products to produce items under the Uniqlo name.

This was the first step towards the development of Uniqlo's SPA (Speciality store retailer of Private label Apparel) business model. Yanai introduced a franchise system and reduced costs even more by buying stock in large quantities. The next step was a point-of-sale (POS) system that used computers to instantly track inventories in the shops and make that information available in the corporate office.

Uniqlo started to gain control over the entire value chain, starting with product development and leading to design, planning, manufacture, distribution, and retail.

This was the beginning of an incredible success story. Uniqlo took a leading role in the improvement of its business model as well as in product design, procurement of raw materials, logistics, and the production of goods. Uniqlo not only responded to changes in consumer needs with improved formats and sales concepts, but introduced innovations along the whole value chain.

The firm adopted strategies very similar to those used by successful Western retailers. For instance, Uniqlo began to focus on selling large quantities of certain articles to achieve economies of scale along the whole chain of production. To do so, attention and resources were focused on selected relatively low-priced items. Uniqlo produces its clothing in China, where labor is cheap, and sells the products exclusively. The quality is good and the clothing inexpensive because the manufacturing is outsourced. Combined with an attractive shipping delivery price agreement, this enables Uniqlo to maintain low prices at the point of sale.

RAW MATERIAL

The chain grew rapidly in size and in 1991 the name of the parent company was changed from Ogori Shoji to Fast Retailing Co. Success was therefore associated with the leadership of Tadashi Yanai. The company grew very fast, reaching 50 stores in 1992. At the same time, all Fast Retailing Co. shops were rebranded as Uniqlo, including the Ogori Shoji shops specializing in formal-wear. Uniqlo focused on selling simple clothing at relatively low prices.

By the beginning of the 1990s, Japanese consumers had changed from luxury shoppers who preferred expensive goods to cost-conscious buyers. The recession that hit Japan after the bubble burst had a powerful impact on Japanese consumer behavior. People suddenly appreciated good quality for a reasonable price. The Japanese retail climate in the 1990s was highly challenging, eventually leading to the downfall of several prominent retailers.

However, Uniqlo benefited from the changes in the market. During the 1990s, the company grew impressively. By April 1994, there were over 100 Uniqlo stores operating throughout Japan. The expansion of Uniqlo's distribution network was funded by its listing on the Hiroshima stock exchange in 1994. By 1997 there were more than 150 Uniqlo shops in Japan and the company was listed on the Tokyo stock exchange.

In the meantime, the company also developed international ambitions. Fast Retailing established a design subsidiary in New York, which was 100% owned by Fast Retailing and aimed to improve design and information collection. To strengthen production, the Japanese retailer established a production subsidiary in Canton, China, in 1996. This subsidiary was a joint venture between five companies, including Nichimen, a general trading company, and other Chinese businesses.

SPLENDID COATS OF MANY COLORS

Despite these various investments, company growth did not occur in a consistent pattern. In the 1990s, with increasing growth and the company's centralization, it became apparent that Uniqlo might suffer from not being able to react quickly to consumer needs and regional differences.

In order to increase sales, Tadashi Yanai decided to focus more on the Uniqlo brand. Up until 1997, Uniqlo stores had sold Uniqlo's brand goods as well as other cheap brands. This marketing strategy was not well understood by employees or customers. Uniqlo's director now redefined the concept, and Uniqlo shops began selling only Uniqlo's brand products. All stores started offering the same service and the same product lines, essentially extending the concept of fast food to clothing. In another bold move, Tadashi Yanai exchanged the existing top management team for a group of experts from other companies. This was one of the youngest management teams in the industry, with an average age of 40, which was very unusual in Japan. This move enabled outlets to have more autonomy.

There were other strategic moves. Originally, the development plan adopted by Yanai and his team involved the accelerated opening of shops in locations with low rent, such as industrial suburbs and stations. It was important for the company to limit the increase of fixed costs arising from such expansion while increasing the "contact points" with consumers. But in 1998, Uniqlo opened its first major urban shop in the Harajuku district of Tokyo, the center of fashion for the city's young people. The Harajuku store's first floor was dedicated to offering fleece clothing in many different colors. This drew shoppers' attention. This was the start of the "fleece boom" which made the company one of the most famous brands in Japan. Uniqlo sold fleece jackets for only 1,900 yen, less than one-fifth of the typical price of other clothing retailers. The response of Japanese customers to the products was very positive. Customers queued in front of Uniqlo stores to get hold of a fleece in one of five sizes. The company sold two million units in just a year. Uniqlo has been a major trendsetter in the domestic casual clothing market ever since. At the beginning, Uniqlo's fleece outfits came in 15 colors. By 2000, the lineup came in 51 shades and the fleece boom continued. In 1999 Uniqlo sold 8.5 million outfits and in 2000 it sold 26 million as the chain's popularity soared.

This success also enabled the firm to establish shops in different locations, widening its sales network. Sales in this period increased by 10%, owing to the opening of new stores. In 1999, the successful Japanese retailer was promoted to the first section of the Tokyo Stock Exchange.

By 2005, Uniqlo had launched more than 700 stores in Japan and had revenue totaling US$3.5 billion. At the same time, Uniqlo, originally a division of the Fast Retailing Co., was re-structured as a separately-owned subsidiary. The company rolled out a new point of sale (POS) platform which enabled faster processing of different applications and reduced support costs. Uniqlo used a system created by the technological company NCR which comprises workstations with touch screens that can process real-time data exchange between stores and the head office. Other tools include analytics and web-based mapping and data transportation technology for store communications. The goal of this partnership for Uniqlo was to run the business faster and more efficiently than ever before. The computer system was introduced to expand the business and to implement the management strategy.

HOT STUFF WITH HEATTECH

In 2003, Uniqlo and Toray Industries Inc., Japan's biggest maker of synthetic fibers, launched a new unique creative line called Heattech. It was the perfect marriage of Japanese technology, impeccable styling, and science. Together, Uniqlo and Toray pursued a comprehensive industrial approach covering all aspects of production from materials to products, as well as planning, development, and logistics. Heattech fibres provide thermal insulation by converting the vapor generated by the body into heat and retaining this heat between micro-thin strands of fiber. Uniqlo's Heattech line was very innovative and spread rapidly across Japan. Brand awareness has increased to 96.3%, according to a random survey of 3,200 people who were asked if they had heard of Heattech. Since its launch, the Heattech line has constantly evolved as Uniqlo incorporates customer feedback to improve product performance and design. The new range is 10% lighter than before, making it even more lightweight and wearable. Moreover, the line offers a wider range of colors, patterns, and design. In 10 years, Uniqlo has sold more than 100 million items around the world from this popular line. In 2008, Uniqlo also started offering Ultra Light Down, a line of warm and lightweight down jackets.

To mark the 10th anniversary of its most popular line, Uniqlo will soon stock a Heattech range for babies alongside the collections for men, women, and children. These thermal-wear products, over time, have become a success story. Originally there was no great demand for the product, but Uniqlo was innovative and went through thousands of iterations in the fabric until it came up with the collection it has today.

Heattech has become the company's bestseller. By 2012 more than 300 million Heattech products had been sold, making thermal underwear one of the most popular products in Japan. 96% of Japanese consumers know the brand, and 55% own a Heattech item.

New Models

Alongside its main brand Uniqlo, the firm also created a second line: g.u. (pronounced jiyuu, which means 'freedom' in Japanese) is a cheaper clothing chain targeting young and trendy Tokyo customers, especially younger women conscious of both fashion and budget. The brand enables people to enjoy fashion without worrying about the price. G.u. has attracted attention by recruiting local stars such as Harajuku fashion princess Kyary Pamyu Pamyu to model in advertising campaigns, and sales are rising. In just six years, g.u.'s turnover passed the 50 billion yen mark. It took the Uniqlo brand about 12 years to do the same.

Brave New World

Having conquered Japan, Uniqlo then focused on its international strategy. Stores were opened in Shanghai and London in 2002. However, poor execution of this expansion meant that the brand was met with indifference by the UK public. This failure did not kill the brand but led to massive improvements in its internationalization processes. Over the following three years, concerted efforts were made to revive and repair the struggling overseas business.

Stores opened in New York, Hong Kong, Seoul, and parts of Europe. At the end of 2011, Uniqlo had 793 stores in Japan, 61 in South Korea, 54 in China, 24 in Taiwan, 16 in Hong Kong, 10 in the UK, seven in Singapore, five in the US, five in Malaysia, four in Thailand, and two each in France, the Philippines and Russia.

As Uniqlo has become a global firm, it has dispersed its operations geographically: there are fashion designers in Tokyo, New York and Paris, garnering first-hand information on fashion trends, while manufacturing departments are located in China to keep costs low. The company's headquarters are still in Japan and strategic decisions are taken there.

The company has also developed a unique corporate culture, using special management tactics called Global One and Zen-in Keiei. They are based on the idea that everyone is a business leader. In Japan, employees are told that they are part of the management, that they make very important decisions, and that they have the potential to make it all the way to the top. Uniqlo hires many people, and spends a lot of time training them. It is something that makes the company distinctive.

UNIQLO: THE BRAND

People often use clothing as a way to express their identity, and brands focus on providing customers with the means to do so. Clothing retail is a sector in which self-expression, fashion, and symbolic value are paramount. These are the principal functions that retailers try to master in order to be successful.

Basic everyday items such as T-shirts, socks and jeans are the less exciting dimensions of the clothing industry, but they are found in almost every wardrobe. Uniqlo, by aiming high, transformed them into a treasure trove.

The impressive range of colors offered is one of Uniqlo's key selling points. Yanai started out with a few different colors, but then asked the question, "Why not 50 colors instead of 10?" It was an innovative and efficient idea appreciated by customers. For Uniqlo, the products themselves are an important source of competitive edge. Uniqlo strives to develop high-quality products in various collections to enable the company to reach the highest possible number of customers.

Customer Care

In its efforts to place the customer first, Uniqlo maintains a clean shop and a full inventory and permits the return of goods for three months from the date of purchase. By keeping strictly to these principles, Fast Retailing considers customer satisfaction its highest priority. Normal concerns held by the average shopper about fashion style, brand identity, and design are assuaged. Uniqlo emphasizes low prices, high quality, and good basic designs that match whatever customers wear. The premise is that consumers can make their own fashion choices; they do not need to have a style dictated to them. The philosophy is to be an "un-branded" fashion retailer. Uniqlo's items are basic and casual but well-made. Its products are affordable, durable, and in a unisex style intended for all ages.

Uniqlo is very sensitive to consumer feedback. It enhances customer satisfaction, since Uniqlo's product development team relies on customers' needs and opinions. Uniqlo's products are designed to incorporate customer requirements and worldwide market trends. The voice of the consumer (VOC) is one of the key requirements of building an effective brand.

TOP QUALITY

Uniqlo has implemented quality control across factory production technology and management. Technical specialists carefully examine production to make sure that the millions of products have a standardized quality. A network of internal blogs allow Uniqlo to collect real-time feedback from its local stores. With mobile phone technology, Uniqlo can tap into the intelligence of its large number of part-time employees who have no computer access.

Uniqlo is more often compared to technology firms than fashion companies. It ignores major fashion trends and focuses on innovative products. So, naturally, some of its management team's biggest influences are technological leaders and companies. CEO Tadashi Yanai has referred to Steve Jobs as an important influence. Uniqlo's management wanted to revolutionize the customer experience. As such, their rivals would be endangered when it came to introducing innovative products. Uniqlo has developed products specifically to meet the needs of customers looking for good value, and focused on developing apparel with value-added functionality such as the Heattech line.

THE NEW SPACE RACE

In addition, Uniqlo has moved towards opening a range of unique stores all over Japan, especially in Tokyo, creating new concepts to provide a better customer experience. Since 2004, Uniqlo has changed its store strategy to emphasize large-format stores with flo-orspace of at least 1,600 square meters. Uniqlo has opened impressive flagship stores to retain a high profile in the market, and holds excit-ing events for store openings, which are always very successful in Japan. These prime urban stores are popular with Japanese customers and generate strong sales. They play an important role in helping to broaden the customer base and further boost the value of the Uniqlo brand. Recently, Uniqlo has opened 25 new large-format stores and closed 23 existing smaller stores.

CONNECTING THREADS

Uniqlo has also been stepping up designer collaborations to boost its brand recognition. For instance, in 2009, it launched a range of new products featuring Disney characters. The company also signed a consulting contract with Jil Sander, a German luxury fashion designer. In a period of slight recession for the Japanese retailer this was an effective boost and the designer offered Uniqlo a new collection called +J that was well-constructed, of good quality, and fairly priced. The partnership, however, ended two years later in 2011.

In another example of successful marketing, Uniqlo provided the uniforms for Japan's Olympic athletes three times — in 1998, 2002, and 2004. In addition, the brand supported the Japanese League Thespa Kusatsu team, a professional football club; and last but not least, Uniqlo has chosen Novak Djokovic, the world's Number 1 male tennis player, as its global brand ambassador for a five-year partnership.

It has also partnered with the giant electronics retailer Bic Camera. Together they have opened a giant outlet called "Bicqlo". The concept is unique and original. The store offers approximately 4,000 square meters of clothes and electronic goods presented side by side. About 4,000 people queued up for the outlet store on its first day. Recently, the Japanese casual clothing brand has expressed its overflowing imagination by opening the Uniqlo Marche Printemps Ginza in Tokyo in November 2012. It is Uniqlo's first ever multi-brand store, offering customers a unique opportunity to peruse five of its most popular labels under one roof. Customers in the store are able to roam approximately 2,600 square meters of retail space showcasing clothing lines from five Fast Retailing Co. brands: G.u. Co., PLST (plus T), Comptoir des Cotonniers, and Princesse tam.tam, alongside its signature Uniqlo brand. "We say that Japan brings the technology and that we bring the French touch," said Delphine Ninous, director of Comptoir des Cotonniers. Indeed, the new line is mainly a version of the ultra-light down jacket created by Uniqlo with an added French feminine twist provided by the French fashion retailer.

Screen Attraction

Yanai's objective is to boost sales by encouraging customers to return regularly to his stores. This is achieved using special offers on basic products and the launch of new, innovative ranges containing cheap products to draw customers in. Once there, they encounter limited series of higher-priced designer clothes. In order to draw customers' attention to these items, Uniqlo has come up with an aggressive marketing campaign. It has hired celebrities (including actors Orlando Bloom and Charlize Theron, and Japanese football player Keisuke Honda) to appear in commercials, and teamed up with popular Japanese fashion magazines and designers in order to create a brand identity.

Networking

Uniqlo, as a progressive company, has incorporated digital strategies in order to communicate with and motivate customers. These strategies do not focus on Japan but are expected to appeal to Japanese consumers as well as the wider world. Uniqlo's move to become an international brand is also influencing its image in Japan. An increasing emphasis has been placed on creative campaigns that include dance, music and the Internet, rather than the spoken word and other traditional forms of marketing. It is a tactic that Uniqlo has adopted to be as inclusive as possible in its approach to consumers and to ensure that existing and potential customers can engage with the company and understand its message, whatever their country of residence.

A YEN FOR SUCCESS

In 2012, Uniqlo was declared Japan's largest clothing retail chain with an impressive network of stores, and with a 5.5% share of the 10.7 trillion yen Japanese clothing market, making Tadashi Yanai the richest man in Japan. By 2020, Fast Retailing Co.'s goal is to achieve 5 trillion yen in sales, and the company also aims to make Uniqlo the world's top clothing chain.

Uniqlo has been successful because of its commitment to diversity, supporting the individuality of each family member, not just those with fashion-forward tastes. Fast Retailing, much like Japan itself, is devoted to simple, functional clothing with minimal detail rather than extravagant, cutting-edge attire. However, the apparel industry is very competitive and Uniqlo's activities have lured a number of fierce rivals into the market. As a result, Uniqlo has lost sales to a growing number of competitors offering similar products such as value-added practical clothing.

The Japanese retailer has had to deal with increasing competition from domestic rivals who have introduced products similar to Uniqlo's Heattech thermal underwear range. Retailers such as Aeon Co., Shimamura Co., and Seven & I Holdings Co. have teamed up to produce their own products offering the same functionality as Uniqlo's thermal underwear.

Uniqlo also faces competition from successful non-Japanese retailers. Today's fashion culture is fast and reactive. Companies such as Zara and H&M are quick to copy any mini-fad that emerges. They also turn over inventory quickly enough to get new clothing onto the sales floor within two weeks. H&M, Zara, and US brands Forever 21 and Gap are often categorized as fast fashion brands, all of which emphasize quick turnover of stock and reasonable prices. They are Uniqlo's main non-Japanese competitors in the Japanese market. Previously, the Japanese consumer was brought up in the firm belief that high prices have to be paid for fashionable designs. While prices for fashionable items have now come down, the quality argument nevertheless remains. Low prices are not the only reason for buying any more; consumers now expect cheap fashion to be high-quality.

These non-Japanese brands are now well established in Japan and they offer fashionable items at lower prices than Uniqlo. For instance, while keeping the H&M brand accessible to the public, H&M is adapting for different customer demographics, winning over Uniqlo's customers little by little. Retail analysts say that Japanese consumers are continuing to spend in the recession, but have gone considerably down-market to less costly items. As a result, fast fashion "is a hot issue in Japan's fashion industry, especially after the entry of H&M," says Dairo Murata, a retail analyst at Credit Suisse in Tokyo.

Uniqlo focuses on technological differentiation, using long product-development cycles and offering basics that appeal to a large consumer base. It identifies styles within product categories that won't quickly go out of fashion, differentiates these styles, and then sets up a supply chain to deliver them to the consumer. It also drives consumers to update their wardrobes because of changes in technology rather than in response to ever-shifting style preferences. In Uniqlo's case, getting customer preferences right is extremely important because of its lengthy development cycles and long-term commitments to materials and products.

In contrast, Zara has built a supply chain that allows it to follow fashion trends and deliver goods almost in real-time. For Zara, reacting to consumer desires is a core component of its competitive advantage, and it has developed a highly responsive supply chain that enables the delivery of new fashions as soon as a trend emerges.

Finally, the Swedish fashion group H&M manages to maintain a commitment to longevity while staying responsive to fashion trends. H&M is well-known for its focus on researching and predicting emerging trends. Both Zara and H&M spring from the "cheap chic" fashion stables of Western Europe, and as such tend to have a trendier image than Uniqlo, which has built its fortune on a platform of functional, less fashion-conscious clothing.

As a consequence of all these factors, Uniqlo can appear over-priced in comparison to other Japanese and foreign fast retailing brands.

HOW TO FIGHT A PRICE WAR

Uniqlo today faces a growing number of strong competitors. The apparel industry is buyer-driven and has low barriers to entry, generating intense competition. This is a challenge for every clothing company. Producers must consider buyers' decisions, especially when brand names enter the picture. In the clothing business, mass customization has been the most effective strategy. Therefore, the focus must be on minimizing the costs without sacrificing quality. Uniqlo understood this concept early and developed strong and effective managerial know-how in order to facilitate creativity and innovation, and to adapt to new market demands and trends. Little by little the company succeeded in building its identity and consumer loyalty. Strengthening a brand name requires quick response programs to manage risks.

At the end of 2010, Fast Retailing Co. forecast that profits that year would fall, mainly due to the struggle to stay competitive in the Japanese market. Fast Retailing declined 9.8% to 11,180 yen on the Tokyo Stock Exchange, a significant drop. Fast Retailing's forecast for 2010 was disappointing, but growing overseas operations are enough at present to make up for slowing sales in Japan.

In September 2011, the company also announced that in the fiscal year that ended on August 31, domestic sales at its own directly operated stores, as well as its sales within each store, fell short of those achieved a year earlier for the first time in eight years.

One response to this has been a renewed focus on Uniqlo's main products. However, Heattech products achieve peak sales in winter and the company does not have a comparable bestseller for the summer. In addition, Uniqlo has also tried to boost its customers' average purchase by getting them more interested in fashionable mid-priced and more expensive products.

But their main strategy is a very risky one. To improve the situation, Uniqlo has entered into a fierce price war with its rivals. For instance, prices have been lowered by 10% and 30% respectively on lines of men's and women's t-shirts. The company offers discounted prices every weekend and is trying to promote its image as a low-cost quality provider of basic fashion.

Lower prices are a concept that has worked very well at the budget chain g.u., but whether the mother brand Uniqlo will succeed is not yet clear. The company urgently needs to develop other less risky growth strategies for its home market.

QUESTIONS

1. What are Uniqlo's success strategies?
2. Did they apply traditional Japanese management practices?
3. Which aspects of their strategies were inspired by other industries?
4. How can they compete successfully against their rivals in Japan?
5. What growth strategies can they develop for international markets?

BIBLIOGRAPHY

Bloomberg — Fast Retailing Forecasts 17% Profit Decline on Slowing Uniqlo Store Sales — by Naoko Fujimura — Oct 2012 http://www.bloomberg.com/news/2010-10-08/fast-retailing-forecasts-annual-profit-will-fall-17-as-uniqlo-sales-slow.html
Business Insider — Uniqlo lesson from Apple — by Kin Bhasin — Oct 2012 http://www.businessinsider.com/uniqlo-lesson-apple-2012-10
Contagious Magazine — Uniqlo Case study by Will Sansom http://www.contagiousmagazine.com/resources/Uniqlo.pdf
Fast Company — Cheap, Chic, And Made For All: How Uniqlo Plans To Take Over Casual Fashion — June 2012 http://www.fastcompany.com/1839302/cheap-chic-and-made-all-how-uniqlo-plans-take-over-casual-fashion
Fast Retailing — Overview of Year to August 2010 and Future Outlook — by Tadashi Yanai http://www.fastretailing.com/eng/ir/library/pdf/20101008_yanai.pdf

Fast Retailing CSR Report 2010 http://www.uniqlo.com/en/csr/report/pdf/csr2012.pdf

Forbes — The Future of Fashion Retailing: Part 1 Uniqlo / Part 2 Zara / Part 3 H&M — by Greg Petro — Oct 2012

Japan Times — Choice, chic, cheap — no one feels fleeced — by Nagata, Kazuaki, November 17, 2009, p. 3. http://www.japantimes.co.jp/text/nn20091117i1.html

Japan Times — Uniqlo teams up with Disney — Sept 2009 http://www.japantimes.co.jp/text/nb20090901a4.html

Japan Times Online — Uniqlo, Bic Camera open joint giant outlet called Bicqlo in Tokyo — by Hiroko Nakata — Sept 2012 http://www.japantimes.co.jp/text/nb20120928a5.html

Nikkei Business — Uniqlo Downplays Domestic slump — by Shintaro Ikeda, Staff Writer, 2001 http://business.nikkeibp.co.jp/article/eng/20110926/222802/

Reading UK — Fast Retailing: An analysis of FDI and supply chain management in fashion retailing by Takahide Yamaguchi and Hiroyuki Yoshida http://www.reading.ac.uk/Econ/Econ/workingpapers/emdp436.pdf

The Wall Street Journal — Uniqlo Operator Boosts Outlook — by Hiroyuki Kachi, Jan 2013

UK essays — Strategic Management at Uniqlo http://www.ukessays.co.uk/essays/business/strategic-management-at-uniqlo.php

Uniqlo.com — Company http://www.uniqlo.com/jp/#!COMPANY

Venture Republic — Uniqlo brand strategy, fashion brand, Japanese brand — by Martin Roll http://www.venturerepublic.com/resources/Uniqlo_brand_strategy_fashion%20brand_Japanese_brand.asp

Vogue — Uniqlo launches New Collaboration — by Ella Alexander — Sept 12 http://www.vogue.co.uk/news/2012/09/10/uniqlo-launches-comptoir-des-cotonniers-collaboration

Wall Street Journal, Japan Real Time Blog: Uniqlo's Hot Thermal Underwear Line Nears 300 Millionth Sale. http://blogs.wsj.com/japanrealtime/2012/09/26/uniqlos-hot-thermal-underwear-line-nears-300-millionth-sale/

Wikipedia — Uniqlo http://en.wikipedia.org/wiki/Uniqlo

The Suntory Highball Revolution: Can a Type of Drink Save an Industry?

Thomas Anderson III

Few corporations become as diverse as Suntory, an enterprise with a large network of group companies ranging from alcoholic beverages to health supplements to restaurant chains. Suntory started off as a small drug store in Osaka at the end of the 19th century and has transformed itself into one of Japan's leading companies in the beverages industry. But even with all these different ventures, Suntory has made a vow to keep pursuing ever higher quality for its products in the industry that really made it what it is today: namely, whisky.

Whisky, a once-thriving market in Japan's 1980s bubble economy, has seen sales declining for over 20 years with no signs of stopping. Not content with its industry-leading 60% share of the decreasing domestic whisky market, Suntory had been trying hard for years to regain customers and spark a turnaround.[1] With the changing demographic in Japan, Suntory felt the need not only to appeal to the "typical" whisky consumer but also to actively target the younger generation to help change its fortunes.

With a long list of failures to reboot the troubled industry, Suntory seemed out of luck and out of options. The challenge had been to make an old product seem new as well as to appeal to a wide

---

[1] M. Ito "Suntory to World: Fancy a drink?" *The Nikkei Weekly*, 18 October 2010, p. 20.

range of consumers. Success didn't start to come until after the re-release of a drink that was popular during the bubble economy, the "whisky highball cocktail," which has recently been credited with reviving the fortunes of the once-dominant whisky distiller. A highball is a mixed drink comprising any type of alcoholic spirit and a non-alcoholic mixer. The most common type of highball is made with Scotch whisky and club soda.[2]

With new marketing and competitive strategies, Suntory, with the help of the highball, seems poised to revive the market: but it may be too early to tell whether it will have long-term success. With past historical proof that whisky can be a hard product to maintain as a long-term staple, the fight for whisky in Japan has only just begun.

THE HISTORY OF SUNTORY AND WHISKY IN JAPAN

Japan's whisky tradition dates back almost 100 years, to the early 1920s, when Masataka Taketsuru studied the art of distilling while in Scotland. Because of these ties to Scotland, the Japanese whisky industry has decided to spell their product without the extra "e." After he returned to Japan he was hired by Suntory's founder Shinjiro Torii to work as their master distiller.[3] In 1923, Japan's first whisky distillery was constructed in Yamazaki on the periphery of former capital Kyoto.[4] During the founding of Suntory,

---

[2] The name "highball" is widely said to have originated in Scotland. Two gentlemen were playing a round of golf when one decided to try a whisky and soda, which was rare in those days. After taking a couple of sips he proceeded to hit his next drive extremely high and deep. The gentlemen, moved by the shot said, "That was a high ball," and the name stuck. (Suntory Holding's Corporate Website. The Delicious Way to Drink Whisky. http://www.suntory.co.jp/whisky/beginner/drink/highball. html. (4 January 2011)).

[3] Locke, Michelle. "Japanese Whisky Invades U.S." *Fox News*, 12 August 2010. http://www. foxnews.com/leisure/2010/08/12/japanese-whisky-invades/. (5 November 2010).

[4] Suntory Holding's Corporate Website. Japan's First Whisky to Achieve the Summit of the Whisky World. http://www.suntory.com/business/liquor/whisky.html. (16 December 2010).

"Shinjiro Torii envisioned a whisky filled with the essence of Japanese nature, hand-crafted by artisans through a patient process of enhancing the work of nature, thus creating a whisky that would suit the palate of the Japanese and perfectly paired with their gastronomy".[5]

It was at Suntory's Yamazaki distillery near Kyoto that Japan's "first genuine domestically distributed whisky," Suntory Shirofuda, or white label, was born. It was not too long after that, in 1937, that their mainstay whisky was introduced, Kakubin, or square bottle. Kakubin remains to this day the most popular seller among their lineup of whiskies. In Shinjiro Torii's pursuit of the perfect whisky a new distillery was opened in Hakushu, strategically located at the foot of Mt. Kaikomagatake in the Southern Japan Alps of Yamanashi Prefecture. Blessed with a unique micro-environment, including untouched forests and water that possesses a softness and rare purity, the Hakushu distillery has produced Suntory's award winning Yamazaki single malt whisky, as well as Hakushu and Hibiki blended whisky.

In 1963 the company changed its name from Kotobukiya to Suntory, and also established its first brewery, now setting its sights on the beer industry as well. In the early 1980s Suntory also acquired Pepcom Industries, which made Suntory the master bottling franchisee for Pepsi-Cola in Japan. At the very end of the 1980s, Suntory launched its soon-to-be mainstay beer, the Premium Malts.[6] All through the 1990s and early 2000s Suntory had remained focused on their whisky development, but was building a well-rounded company on the side. They looked to further development of the market for soda and other canned beverages and started to get into the medicine and health-supplement industry.[7]

---

[5] The Art of Japanese Whisky. The Art of Japanese People. *Azukaru, Takusu, Awaseru*: To Be Bestowed With, to Pass on, and to Blend. http://www.suntory.com/whisky/en/philosophy/people.html. (8 December 2010.)

[6] Suntory Holding's Corporate Website. "History of SUNTORY." http://www.suntory.com/history/index02.html. (4 January 2011).

[7] Suntory Holdings Corporate Website. "History of SUNTORY." http://www.suntory.com/history/index03.html. (4 January 2011).

Sales by business segment

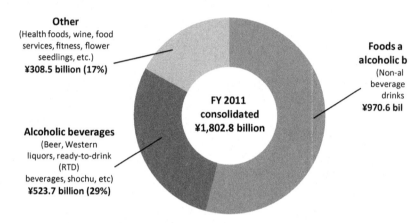

Other
(Health foods, wine, food services, fitness, flower seedlings, etc.)
¥308.5 billion (17%)

Foods a alcoholic b
(Non-al beverage drinks
¥970.6 bil

FY 2011
consolidated
¥1,802.8 billion

Alcoholic beverages
(Beer, Western liquors, ready-to-drink (RTD) beverages, shochu, etc)
¥523.7 billion (29%)

Fig. 1   Sales by business segment.

Suntory has a hand in a wide range of businesses and has been successful to the point that over half of their revenue comes from outside their original alcoholic beverage industry (see Fig. 1[8]).

Although they are making most money from their foods and non-alcoholic beverage endeavors, Suntory's image in the eyes of the consumer is that of a distributor of alcoholic beverages, specifically whisky and beer. Suntory has placed emphasis on whisky since the beginning, and remains enthusiastic about trying to create a large, stable market for whisky in Japan well into the 21st century.

In 2004 Japan's domestic whisky market had clearly seen better days and was selling around 10 million cases a year, down from 1983 when it was selling over four times as much (45 million cases per year). Suntory's sales of whisky in 2004 were sitting at a meager 5.6 million cases. No matter what they tried, whether new drinks or creative marketing, they could not get their sales to stop dropping.

In 2004, Suntory's was to employ "Chemistry," a Japanese J-Pop and R&B duo, to star in their commercials; one commercial had them

---

[8] Suntory Holdings Corporate Website. Corporate Overview. http://www.suntory.com/profile/index.html. (25 June 2012).

performing live at one of Suntory's distilleries. They also tried to push a new way of drinking whisky, the Half Rock, which is half whisky and half water or soda on the rocks.[9] They were hoping that the younger generation would think that this way of drinking whisky would come across as more fashionable and stylish and finally break them out of their cold spell.[10]

Suntory believed that the reason the younger generation was not drinking whisky was not due to their turning away from alcohol but because they had fewer opportunities to drink whisky as opposed to more common and cheaper drinks such as beer and *Chu-hais*, a canned ready-to-drink (RTD) beverage made of Japanese *shochu* and soda water. Suntory tried to allow younger people more chances to drink whisky by running promotions offering a free shot of whisky and even outfitting one of their distilleries with Christmas lights to lure in potential consumers. Suntory can hardly be blamed for lack of effort, but in the end all their concepts and promotions were for naught: sales continued to slide, to under 10 million cases market-wide, and with Suntory falling to about 5.4 million cases in the following year.

SUCCESS IN FOREIGN MARKETS

With campaigns not working at home, Suntory had to start looking abroad to increase sales of their product. Suntory's ultimate goal is to make its high-end whiskies known throughout the world on the same scale as major Scottish labels. But as Eric Ariyoshi, a Suntory brand manager in San Francisco, is quick to point out, Suntory wants the world to know that their whisky is "not Scotch made in Japan" but a uniquely Japanese product. One focus point is China: due to its rapid economic growth and increasingly more open trade, Suntory is working

---

[9] Suntory Holding's Corporate Website. The Delicious Way to Drink Whisky. http://www.suntory.co.jp/whisky/beginner/drink/half.html. (8 December 2010).
[10] Japan Consumer Marketing Research Institute (2005). *Uisuki shijo fukkatsu naru ka — moruto ninki wo tsuujita santori no wakamonozou kouryaku* [Can the whisky market rebound? Suntory's strategy for the younger generation], p. 2.

hard to create a whisky culture in China's big cities, targeting the fast-growing class of affluent Chinese consumers.[11]

On September 14th, 2010 Suntory held a dinner in Paris at the Japanese ambassador's house with about 60 business leaders and other well-known Frenchmen. Executive general manager Tetsu Mizutani said "The event was designed to give influential individuals a taste of Suntory whiskies in hopes of building their reputation by word of mouth." Suntory is planning on holding more events like this in other Western countries.

The annual sales of Suntory's Yamazaki totaled about 180,000 cases including sales both in and outside Japan, making it the world's eighth best-selling single malt. In 2010, Suntory was hoping to sell 8,000 cases of Hibiki and 31,000 cases of Yamazaki in overseas markets. These numbers, however, pale in comparison to the 46.5 million cases total of all whisky sales in the United States in 2009, according to statistics from the US Distilled Spirits Council, showing that there is a lot of potential in overseas markets.

Although the quantity of Suntory's high-end whisky has not yet reached its potential, its product is winning quality awards around the world. Since 2003, all three of Suntory's high-end whiskies have won awards at various competitions. Every year, Whisky Magazine holds its "Icons of Whisky Awards" honoring companies and distillers from around the globe: for 2010, Suntory won the Distiller of the Year award, which was the first for a Japanese corporation.[12]

But even with this success abroad, there was none to be found in Japan. This was due to factors pertaining to both the younger generation and the baby-boom generation. The younger generation is supposedly not drinking as much alcohol, while the baby-boom generation has been hard hit by the economy and so keeps a tighter grip

---

[11] Suntory Holding's Corporate Website. Building Premium Alcoholic Beverages around the World. http://www.suntory.com/business/liquor/global.html. (8 December 2010).

[12] Whisky Magazine. Icons of Whisky. http://www.whiskymag.com/awards/icons_of_whisky/2010/. (8 December 2010).

on their wallets; thus they are less willing or less able to purchase the international-award-winning premium whisky that Suntory offers.

In 2006 Suntory's sales were lower than they had ever been; Suntory was desperate to turn around their fortunes but many problems stood in their way. For years, not only Suntory but the whole industry had been plagued with the image of whisky being an alcohol only drunk by an older generation of men, in their forties and above. Suntory also had to deal with the fact that the Japanese economy had been struggling for over 20 years and people had less money to spend — or at least less money that they were willing to spend — on expensive spirits such as whisky.

On top of whisky's old man image, their main target — the "young generation," which Suntory defines as both men and women in their twenties — was said to be going through a phenomenon called *sake banare* where they were drinking less and less alcohol. Men and women in their twenties are experiencing one of the worst periods for finding a job in the recent history of Japan. Without a job and thus lacking the type of community that work brings, young people are unlikely to go out drinking with their *senpais*, or superiors. Hisakazu Matsuda believes that without these opportunities younger people have very few chances to be introduced to spirits such as whisky, and will never be able to "overcome" the taste if they try it alone and do not like it.[13] Year 2006 presented a grim scene for Suntory and the whisky industry as a whole.

SUNTORY'S SAVIOR: THE HIGHBALL

Although Suntory is producing world-class whisky, it feared losing its iron-clad grip on the domestic whisky market. With none of the past attempts having had any effect on the Japanese consumers, Suntory returned to a past favorite to help and win back the masses. After 20 to 30 years of its lying dormant, they brought the whisky highball back from the dead: this has single-handedly been helping them to

---

[13] H. Matsuda "*Kawanai riyuu, kawareru houhou*" [The reason they don't buy, how to make them buy]. September 30, 2010. Asahi Shimbun Publications Inc.

restore life into the whisky industry as a whole.[14] The whisky high-ball, as mentioned earlier, is a drink made of whisky and club soda. But this time around Suntory has made a lot of moves to ensure their currently rejuvenated brand image stays fresh, allowing the consumer more than ample opportunities to drink and become familiar with the product.

Sales of beer have been decreasing for the last five consecutive years, which has given Suntory and their whisky a chance to turn some consumers on to their product. Alongside beer's decline, the sales of whisky — with the help of the highball — have been increasing. Highballs first started to become popular due to its consumption in local *izakayas* (Japanese pubs) and bars. Mr. Fujita, a bar manager in Osaka, says that almost half of his customers order highballs due to the crispness of the carbonation. He has even gone as far as to install one of Suntory's Highball Towers in his bar right next to the draft beer. The Highball Tower is a contraption that contains club soda and Suntory's Premium Malts beer side-by-side. Once the club soda is ready the bartender then pours in Suntory's Kakubin whisky to finish off the creation.[15] The number of Highball Towers is still fairly limited, but they have increased in popularity. As the whisky highball gains recognition, the number of restaurants serving them is increasing. In 2009 there were about 60,000 restaurants and bars that served highballs on their menu; in 2010 that number more than doubled to 130,000 establishments.[16]

---

[14] Sankei Shimbun. "*Haibo-ru ninki de uisuki- fukken. Santori- 11 nenburi zousan*" [Whisky's revival at the hands of the highball. Suntory to increase production for first time in 11 years]. September 22, 2009. http://www.sankei-kansai.com/2009/09/22/20090922-014915.php. (2 October 2010).

[15] *Ibid.*

[16] Suntory Holding's Corporate Website. Alcoholic Beverages Business Strategy for 2011. January 11, 2011. http://www.suntory.co.jp/news/2011/10974.html. (15 January 2011).

Recently, highballs have also come in canned forms, which have steadily become a regular product at convenience stores — taking precious shelf space from *chu-hais*. Even so, Ready-to-Drink (RTD) highballs offered in cans have a long way to go to achieve market parity, as the consumption rate of *chu-hais* is still about 20 times higher than that of highballs.[17] The cans are aimed at consumers who wish to pick one up at the convenience store on the way home and have it that evening with dinner. A representative from Takara Shuzo, an alcoholic beverage producer headquartered in Kyoto, believes that the reason for the success of the highball-style drinks is due to the trend for more people to go home to eat during the economic downturn, and the fact that the drinks seem to go very well with many foods. Now that the highballs have been made available in an RTD can, the consumers are no longer faced with the labor of making their own drinks and can have one anytime, anywhere. In a report released

Fig. 2 Whisky highball RTD cans sandwiched in between beer and chu-hai (Author).

---

[17] G. Suzuki. "*Santori- no uisuki- zekkouchou! Samenu haibo-ru ninki no koujunkan*" [Suntory whisky hitting full stride! The continuing pleasant circle of popular highballs]. May 21, 2010. Retrieved at http://diamond.jp/articles/-/4407. (2 October 2010).

by Suntory, at least one in four people had consumed an RTD highball can in the previous year. In another survey on the image of the RTD highball cans, Suntory found that around 33% of people believed that the RTD highball cans were for men, while 30% thought that they were a big seller.[18]

Even though Suntory and their highballs are riding a high right now, Suntory Liquor Division's president Yasunori Aiba is aware that they have lost the market once before, 25 years ago, and that they need to maintain control to see that this does not happen again. Mr. Aiba is hoping that highballs will be a so-called "entry good," leading drinkers to buy the more expensive, high-end brands such as Yamazaki and Hibiki.

THE HIGHBALL CRAZE IN JAPAN

One of Suntory's strategies this time around was to work not only on the young generation but the older generation as well. With the younger generation they were focusing on conveying a feeling of a fresh, new style of drink that would hopefully lead to them trying some of the more expensive whiskies. For the older generation, Suntory was hoping to reintroduce a product that would allow them to bask in the nostalgia of the "good old days" when the economy was at full speed and the highball was a staple drink.

Suntory has been very active in making actress Koyuki the face of the highball revolution. Koyuki is probably most famous outside Japan for playing the lead female role in the 2003 blockbuster, The Last Samurai, alongside Tom Cruise. Using such a notable actress has allowed them to penetrate into the younger generation's awareness and raise the recognition of the brand. Suntory has used their mainstay whisky, Kakubin, in all of the commercials featuring Koyuki. The majority of commercials have her behind the bar taking orders from younger patrons who look as if they are done with a long day's

[18] Suntory Holding's Corporate Website. Consumer Research Regarding Suntory's RTD Alcoholic Beverages 2011. http://www.suntory.co.jp/news/2011/11000.html. (27 January 2011).

Fig. 3 Kakubin and Tory's Extra whisky neatly shelved with club soda at a Japanese supermarket (Author)

work. After taking orders and cooking, the commercials end with her making and drinking a Kakubin highball. There are also variations on the commercial that have Koyuki alone at a table with the ingredients to make a highball. In these commercials she guides the viewer through a "seminar" on Suntory's recommended way of creating the perfect highball. Suntory has also created new commercials for special occasions such as Father's Day. In one particular ad it suggests the best present a father can get is time spent with his children; the commercial then suggests that you invite your father over for a highball every now and then. These commercials have helped to raise recognition of highballs to a new level; company employees have instructions on "how to make a delicious highball" embossed on the back of their business cards.

In the background to all of the commercials we hear the song "*Uisuki ga osuki desho*" (You like whisky, don't you?), which has become synonymous with the Kakubin highballs. So synonymous, in fact, that in July 2010 Suntory collaborated with Japan Rail East Company to change the melody that plays before a train departs Shimbashi station to the song. Suntory considers Shimbashi to be the

Fig. 4 Suntory highball bar in Shimbashi, Tokyo (Author)

izakaya holy land, where salary men would go out for a drink after work.[19] This has enticed Suntory to create a highball-based bar about a minute's walk from Shimbashi station. The Highball Bar Shimbashi 1923 has a "nostalgic modern" theme and hopes to provide an old-fashioned relaxing atmosphere where Suntory can promote their higher-end products (See Fig. 4).[20]

THE WHISKY HIGHBALL'S APPEAL

The appeal of whisky highballs is plentiful, according to a study done by Suntory. There are four points why whisky appeals to the health-conscious consumer. First, the amount of calories in whisky is low

---

[19] Asahi Shimbun. *Shimbashi de uisuki-ga suki desho = hassha merodi-, koukoku ni JR higashi* [You like whisky, don't you? Turned into the train melody at Shimbashi station]. http://www.asahi.com/national/jiji/JJT201007210003.html. (16 December 2010).

[20] Suntory Holding's Corporate Website. "*Haibo-ru senmon no shingitai HIGHBALL BAR wo kaihatsu*" [A highball specialty bar opens]. http://www.suntory.co.jp/news/2011/10976.html. (20 January 2011).

compared to other drinks such as beer. Second, it contains almost no purines, which increase the risk of gout. Third, polyphenols are included, which have a variety of health benefits ranging from being an antioxidant to helping fight tooth decay. Lastly, Suntory says that the smell of whisky has been proved to help the consumer relax when drinking it.[21]

Another reason the highball is so attractive is its taste. The younger generation is having a tough time getting used to the bitterness and sharpness of beer, so in many situations they have decided to go with sweeter options, such as sweeter alcoholic beverages like *chuhai* and now, conveniently, whisky highballs with added citrus.

One aspect of the highball that is favored by all is the price. In the current economic slump consumers going to bars and *izakayas* are able to order highballs for less money than a beer of the same size. The prospect of economizing thus adds another reason to drink the highball. On the other side of the transaction, the bar owners like the whisky highballs because the cost of providing one is about 51–100 yen lower than providing the same amount of beer. This gives them a bigger profit margin, which is one of the reasons why the number of establishments serving whisky highballs has increased so quickly.

JUMPING ON THE HIGHBALL BANDWAGON

Suntory has two main competitors when it comes to the whisky market: Nikka Whisky, which is run by Asahi Breweries, and Kirin Brewery. Since the success of Suntory's Kakubin highball, both have made attempts to get their piece of the highball boom. Much like Suntory, they have been combining products with club soda to appeal to the highball crowd. They have also both released RTD canned highballs. Kirin released "The World's Highball"[22] in 2009

[21] Suntory's Customer Support Page. Retrieved at http://www.suntory.co.jp/customer/faq/001777.html. (23 November 2010).
[22] Kirin Brewery Company Corporate Website. "The World's Highball: New Release." http://www.kirin.co.jp/company/news/2009/1125_01.html. (15 January 2011).

and two separate highballs in late 2010, based on American whisky. Nikka released an RTD canned highball based on Masataka Taketsuru, the founder of Japanese whisky and the Nikka Distillery, in late 2010.[23] Although more competitors are beginning to enter the market, it is still limited to the few main breweries.

Suntory has also released a competitor, if you will, in the form of Tory's Extra. Tory's has been around since its re-release following the Second World War, but now Suntory has been ramping up advertising to try and pull even more consumers into the highball boom. On 19 September 2010 the new Tory's Extra was released, along with a RTD highball can.[24] Upon its release, 'Tory's Highball can' quickly took the top spot in number of shares in the RTD cocktail drink market. It jumped ahead of the Kaku highball can after only one week, and as of the third week of October was maintaining a solid 12.5% share of the market.[25] Selling for about 30 yen less per can than Kakubin, Tory's canned highball is said by some to be a step down in taste — which raises the question: Do consumers really care about the taste?[26]

IS THE HIGHBALL A FAD?

The Japanese highball trend seems to be on track to stay for a long time, and it seems as if nothing could be going better for industry leader Suntory. They have had two back-to-back years of large growth in their whisky department, seeing overall whisky sales rise 17%. But

---

[23] Asahi Breweries' Corporate Website. "Taketsuru Premium Highball: News Release." http://www.asahibeer.co.jp/news/2010/1019_2.html. (15 January 2011.)

[24] Suntory Holding's Corporate Website. "Tory's (Extra) Tory's Highball Can New Release." July 20, 2010. http://www.suntory.co.jp/news/2010/10818.html. (15 January 2011).

[25] Nikkei Marketing "The Ups and Downs of Store Goods: Cocktail Drinks." *Nikkei Marketing Journal*, 1 November 2010, 2.

[26] Suntory Holding's Corporate Website. "Suntory Kaku Highball 350 Can, New Release." September 8, 2009. http://www.suntory.co.jp/news/2009/10551.html. (15 January 2011).

they have one problem: no one is making the hoped-for leap from the cheap whisky used in highballs to the more expensive premium products. They continue to struggle to persuade frugal Japanese consumers to switch over, which is what will be needed to maintain growth in the long run. In Japan, buying habits are typical of a collectivist-oriented culture, and one of the collectivist features often represented in Japanese consumer behavior is the fad. "Pack consumerism" has been instilled by peer pressure since childhood and drives the desire to conform; this is why it is believed that Japanese are so prone to fads. An example of a fad in Japan was the panda craze of 1972, when two pandas arrived from China.[27]

A more recent example is that of *taberu rayu*, an edible hot pepper oil and a spicy food condiment that was used to top rice and other food items. *Taberu rayu* was not a new product, but was lifted to the number three spot on the Nikkei Business Special on 2010's hit products thanks to Japanese pack consumerism.[28] Fickle, fad-obsessed Japanese consumers may decide that the highball craze is over at any time: and most of Suntory's current customer base would thus disappear.

In 2012 the Suntory Group worked to increase the demand for its liquor products both in Japan and abroad by ongoing reinforcement of its product value showcasing and marketing activities, centering on Kakubin whisky as well their Premium Malts beer.[29] To remain a leader in the alcoholic beverage industry Suntory must continue their aggressive marketing strategies for whisky and continue to make their products attractive, while offering value to the consumer. They must also focus on creating a more fluid transition to the premium whisky brands for consumers whose interests have been

---

[27] P. Haghirian and A. Toussaint (2011). "Japanese Consumer Behavior," in P. Haghirian (ed.), *Japanese Consumer Dynamics* (New York: Palgrave Macmillian), pp. 11–30.

[28] Nikkei Business. "(*Nichijou ni uruoi*) *wo kau tokushu 2010 nen hitto syouhin ranking*" [(Gain Everyday) Special Collection of 2010's Hit Goods Ranking], December 21–27, 2010, p. 33.

[29] Suntory Holding's Corporate Website. The Delicious Way to Drink Whisky. http://www.suntory.co.jp/whisky/beginner/drink/half.html. (8 December 2010).

stimulated by the highballs, if they hope to maintain their current fortunes. For a company setting its sights on the world, they must start at home and get a firm grip on the domestic market before they can expect to become one of the world's leaders in whisky. Although their hopes are high, Suntory's quest is only just beginning, and their true test lies ahead of them.

QUESTIONS

1. Which strategies can the company develop to implement a long-lasting consumer attitudes change?
2. Will the introduction of the highball also be successful in other Asian markets?
3. Which particularities of the Japanese consumer market can you recognize?
4. Can Japanese marketing practices also be successful in Western countries?

A Tale of Three Companies: The Survival Strategies of Sony, Hitachi, and Canon

David Trappolini

After World War II, Japan was still developing economically and nobody could have predicted the economic success that the country would go on to achieve.

A major player in this process of development was Japan's electronics industry. After the war, many firms were created in the field of technology, and they started to develop consumer electronics products. They quickly became large exporters, beating their foreign competitors with hardware breakthroughs and high-quality products. They have been responsible for huge advances concerning such things as lasers, diodes, screens, and semiconductors. By driving down their manufacturing costs thanks to cheap labor, and copying the designs of Western products, these companies overpowered the US consumer electronics industry.

By 1985, Japan was exporting more color televisions than the US. The Japanese companies pushed the limits of technological development by creating the most advanced products while moving the manufacture of basic components to developing countries. In the late 1990s, the demand for electronic gadgets was very high. The Internet and personal computer use were exploding all over the world. This trend, combined with a depreciating yen, saw Japanese firms earning fortunes. Thus, Japan became the world hub of high-tech electronics.

THE JAPANESE MANAGEMENT SYSTEM

The success of these electronics companies was based on traditional Japanese management practices, which differ greatly from Western business approaches. The main objectives of Japanese firms are stability and cooperation. Japanese corporations also have a strong focus on processes and procedures, which should be performed as carefully as possible. This idea is based on the traditional samurai code of *Bushido*, in which performing one's task at the highest level is considered a virtue.

The principle that processes must be performed with great care and patience was very useful for Japanese firms during the period of rapid economic development. Since many Japanese firms were only just starting out in manufacturing, they had the opportunity to improve and perfect operation and production processes.

In Japanese, the term "manufacturing" translates as *monozukuri*, literally "making things." Many Japanese corporations, for example Toyota, have become world leaders in cost-effective and high-quality production. This dedication to process has also helped Japan's electronics firms to create outstanding products that are often the world's thinnest and smallest.

Monozukuri is a source of national pride and the spirit of craftsmanship is held responsible for the post-war success of large Japanese firms such as Panasonic and Sony.[1] However, many Japanese corporations are thought to focus too much on producing the best quality, and are criticized for losing track of consumers' wishes with regards to newer designs and innovative products.

Another aspect of Japanese human resource management is lifetime employment. Japanese people employed under this system enter a life of dedicated service to one company, and job transfers are neither socially acceptable nor desirable. Many Japanese believe that

---

[1] D. Wakabayashi, and M. Inada (2010). Questions grow on Japanese manufacturing quality. *Wall Street Journal*, 29 January 2010.

this approach is also responsible for the impressive rise of Japanese firms as world-class competitors.[2] For example, all workers start by solving problems at a grass-roots level, which provides them with useful basic knowledge, and the involvement of employees in the company is subsequently boosted *via* specific training. This philosophy also encourages information-sharing between different generations and hierarchical levels; but lifetime employment is by no means an unmixed blessing for firms.[3]

Lifetime employment has also resulted in another aspect of Japanese corporate culture: seniority-based wages. As the name suggests, the salary of workers increases on the basis of age and not merit. Unfortunately, however, this system does not reward employees who perform better, and in a world where emerging countries are becoming very aggressive, this is a competitive disadvantage. Reform here could enhance the competitiveness of Japanese firms.[4]

A central pillar of the Japanese economy and perhaps its most defining characteristic is the *keiretsu* structure of many manufacturing firms. *Keiretsu* is the term for a conglomerate or financial group. Traditionally, *keiretsu* are vertically organized, consisting of many small-and medium-sized businesses that come together to form one unified company. The firms are often centered around a large bank.

Keiretsu have been a key element of Japan's rapid industrial development and transformation since the early 1950s.[5] A *keiretsu* consists of a set of companies with interlocking business relationships and shareholdings. The companies each own a small portion of the shares. The result is the creation of a huge conglomerate that grows slowly, and by taking few risks. Its structure protects the members from foreign takeover and market fluctuation; since they have tied their fates together,

---

[2] R. Kambayashi and T. Kato (2008). *The Japanese Employment System after the Bubble Burst: New Evidence.*

[3] H. Tabushi (2009). *In Japan, Secure Jobs Have a Cost.* (www.nytimes.com/2009/05/20/business/global/20zombie.html?_r=2&). [14 June 2013]

[4] K. Endo (2006). *Pay System and Employment Practice of the Japanese Firm in Transition.*

[5] K. E. Calder (1993). *Strategic Capitalism: Private Business and Public Purpose in Japanese Industrial Finance.* Princeton: University Press.

when stocks for one company in the group grow, they will all grow, and when losses are incurred, they can be split between all the members. However, such structures are very static and are slow to react in a crisis.[6]

Another important factor in the rapid economic development of Japan and its electronic firms is the Japanese work ethic and focus on achievement. One of the highest virtues is that of doing one's best, persisting, and working hard. *Ganbaru* is an active process wherein one works hard in pursuit of a goal, strives to overcome difficulties that might arise, and takes on difficult tasks even though they might be arduous. It also embodies the philosophy of transforming one's future and status by one's own efforts, regardless of personal background.

THE PRESENT JAPANESE ELECTRONICS INDUSTRY

Since the start of the 21st century, many Japanese electronics companies have struggled with financial problems. Foreign companies from South Korea and Taiwan are capable of improving their products more quickly and are able to manufacture more user-friendly goods. Thanks to a more effective marketing strategy, they now lead in many sectors, including Japan's former fiefdoms of TVs and computers. In 2009, after the financial crisis, Samsung Electronics had an operating profit twice as large as the combined profit of nine of Japan's largest consumer electronics companies.

Sharp is a good example of this decline. The company that invented LCD technology announced record losses for 2012, and the chairman expressed severe doubts about the survival of the company. Similarly Renesas, the Japanese manufacturer of semiconductors, will have to be bailed out by the Japanese government to avoid bankruptcy. Finally Nintendo, the legendary videogames company, announced the first loss in its history in 2012.

Much ink has been spilled in the attempt to explain this decline. Japanese managers are inclined to blame the strong yen, which makes

---

[6]S. Howard *et al.* (2002). Global strategy lessons from Japanese and Korean business groups. *Business Horizons*, March–April 2002.

it more difficult to export goods. This is a problem that does not affect Korean firms, which have fewer problems with a strong currency. They can manufacture products almost as well as their Japanese counterparts, but at a much lower price. Other factors such as the Fukushima disaster, and the flood in Thailand, where many Japanese factories are located, are also considered factors in the decline. More recently, territorial tensions with China led to a boycott of Japanese products that affected the turnover of many electronics firms.

Despite this deterioration, in 2013 Japan is still a pillar in the field of technology. Japanese companies no longer dominate the sector as they did before, but some remain significant players in the electronics industry. These include Hitachi, Sony, Nikon, Canon, NEC, Nintendo, Panasonic, Olympus, Sharp, Toshiba, and many others. It would be too simplistic to say that these companies, with their glorious histories, are now simply outdated. Indeed, a recent study conducted by an electronic appliances analyst concluded that Japanese firms make more than half of the components used in the iPhone 5. Sony, Toshiba, and Sharp provide goods such as camera image sensors, memory devices, and display panels to the world leader in technology, Apple.

JAPANESE CRISIS MANAGEMENT

Nevertheless, we cannot deny that the Japanese electronics industry as a whole is on a downward slope. Most firms in Japan share the features mentioned above, and so have been exposed to the same problems in recent years. However, they have not all reacted in the same way. The world economic crisis has made Japanese business leaders think about new ways to adapt in a world where the competition is increasingly global. Japanese firms all prefer Japanese management styles, but many of them have realized that they need to change and adapt faster to the rapidly evolving international business environment.

And they have not all chosen the same strategies. The next sections will describe the cases of three major players in the Japanese electronics industry, as well as their survival strategies: these are Sony, Hitachi, and Canon. Despite similar roots, they are all attempting to adjust their businesses in different ways in a global market full of challenges and opportunities.

SONY

History

On May 7, 1946, Masaru Ibuka (an engineer) and Akio Morita (a physicist) invested the equivalent of 190,000 yen to start a company with just 20 employees. It was called "Tokyo Tsushin Kogyo" and was established in Nihonbashi in Tokyo. The company initially specialized in research and manufacturing of telecommunications and measuring equipment. The name "SONY" came later and was created by combining *sonus,* which is Latin for "sonic," with "sonny," meaning a youthful boy with a free and innovative spirit. It was chosen for its simple pronunciation that could be easily articulated in any language. The new name perfectly suited the company, which wanted to project the image of a group of young people with energy and passion for unlimited creation.

Sony developed strongly after 1954, when the company obtained a license to produce transistors, a basic electronic component which had been invented in America six years before. The following year it began selling the first radio receptor made entirely with transistors. In 1960, Sony America was created, and shortly after, the company opened subsidiaries in Hong Kong and Switzerland. Six years later, as a symbol of power, the Sony building was opened in the luxurious Ginza district of Tokyo: this was a showroom dedicated to the products of the brand.

In terms of innovation, the decades that followed made Sony a global leader. In 1971, the company launched the first color video-cassette, and in 1975 the video recorder Betamax. Amongst Sony's greatest inventions is the famous Walkman, invented in 1979, which led to a real change in music listening habits. For the first time, music became easily portable. It also introduced the idea of miniaturization and high technology, an image that would later become strongly associated with Japan. Some years later, Sony also released the Betacam, the first camcorder for the general consumer. In 1985, the company started to sell the first digital video recorder and in 1994 it became the world leader in the video games industry with the launch of the PlayStation. In 2004, Sony's turnover reached 69 billion euros and its share in the global consumer electronics industry was more than 14%. More recently, in 2006, the company succeeded in implementing Blu-Ray as the standard high-definition format and three years later released the world's first OLED TV. Today, Sony is still one of the most prominent manufacturers of electronics products for consumers and professionals. The company remains very active, launching many new electronics devices every year. Its headquarters are based in the Minato district of Tokyo.

Sony has diversified into several types of activity over time. Figure 1 shows the weight of each business unit in 2012.

SONY TODAY

"That's our coming back." These few words were uttered at the Consumer Electronics Show in Las Vegas — the world conference on electronics — by Kazuo Hirai, the CEO of Sony. The Japanese company delivered a demonstration of advanced technology during the conference by presenting its new Xperia Z[7], a powerful Android smartphone offering technical features to rival any of its competitors. Sony has put all its technological know-how regarding cameras, full

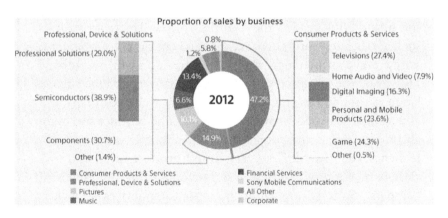

Fig. 1   Sony's business units.

(*Source*: Sony's annual report 2012)

[7] See Appendix for more details.

HD screens, and NFC[8] into its new flagship device. Sony is determined to scare its biggest rivals, Apple and Samsung. However, so far the US and South Korean giants do not have much to fear from Sony. Indeed, they are making record profits year after year, while Sony is losing market share in many sectors and is facing major financial problems. Looking at the evolution of Sony's stock, its price recently hit its lowest point in 30 years (see Appendix). Sony's market valuation is now at $11 billion, a lightweight compared to Apple and Samsung, which are respectively worth $480 and $176.5 billion. The group has also made a net loss in the past four years, with a net deterioration since 2011 (see Appendix), mainly due to the poor performance of the TV department. The aggressive price war led by South Korean companies has resulted in losses for eight consecutive years in this division. Despite these results, Sony has no wish to abandon its TV activities and the management is targeting a return to profitability in the short term. In 2012, Sony shares were downgraded to junk status by rating agency Fitch.

An interesting anecdote about Sony

In 2004, the group, in an attempt to be innovative, launched the first e-book reader, the "Librie." Some American analysts, such as Michael Gartenberg, saw this invention as a harbinger of a new wave of products that could be successful worldwide. However, the product suffered from many problems such as language limitations (the product was only available in Japanese) and a small selection of available books. The product was a flop and Sony halted the project in 2007. Shortly after, Amazon launched the "Kindle," an easy-to-use product offering a wide variety of content. Success was immediate for the American company. Sony is now launching successor devices to make a comeback, but will have to fight to keep a thin market.

---

[8] NFC: Near Field Communication is a set of standards for smartphones to establish radio communication with each other by bringing them into close proximity.

Survival Strategies

In order to become profitable again, Sony is making changes to its business units. A new plan is intended to cut 6% of the total employees of the group before March 2013. Kazuo Hirai wants to focus on three activities and increase the interconnectivity between the consumer goods of the company. Digital imaging, games, and mobile technology will be the spearheads of the group in the upcoming years. They are projected to generate 85% of the company's operating income in 2015. As for the other sectors, the firm plans to either abandon them or create partnerships with other companies.

On October 27, 2011, Sony took full control of Sony Ericsson, a joint venture producing mobile phones, created 10 years earlier by the then-separate companies, Sony and Ericsson. They plan to move the subsidiary from Sweden to Tokyo in order to speed up the decision-making process. The group wants to take a major role in the smartphone market, led by Apple, of which it missed the start. To achieve this, Sony will rely heavily on its smartphone line, "Xperia." The name is derived from the word "experience," and the first phone in this line was released in 2008. The start of the Xperia line was rather disappointing, but Sony is now developing the connection between its smartphones and other forms of media to increase the attractiveness of the phone. By transferring Sony Entertainment Network to its Xperia line, Sony will be able to promote its movies, music, and games to the users of the phones.

Concerning its TV division, Sony ended the joint venture in LCD technology with Samsung in December 2011. This operation is part of a plan to drastically reduce the costs of the TV branch. The company is also making strategic alliances to develop new technology quicker and more efficiently. On June 25, 2012, Sony announced a partnership with Panasonic to jointly develop the next-generation display OLED.[9] This uses less power while providing a better quality image.

---

[9] OLED: Organic light-emitting diode.

On July 2, 2012, Sony announced that it had acquired Gaikai Inc., the world leader in cloud-gaming. According to Andrew House, CEO of Sony Computer Entertainment, this acquisition was made to combine the technological strength of Gaikai with Sony's gaming platform to provide new experiences for consumers. This partnership may be profitable for many Sony products such as the Playstation, Playstation Portable, and the smartphones.

In September 2012, Sony bought shares of 11.46% in Olympus, a major player in the digital imaging sector. The objective was to gain access to the technology of its medical equipment division, a market expected to reach 7.5 billion euros within 10 years. Hirai wants to continue to pursue merger and acquisitions opportunities in the medical sphere. Sony can benefit from its strengths in digital imaging technologies in order to gain a significant competitive advantage in this sector.

Sony's smallest business units have also been included in the restructuring. For example, Sony's chemical products business was recently sold off, and similarly, in the field of automotive battery and energy storage, Hirai said that the group needed to change the current situation because it had several shortcomings.

The group is also increasing its presence in emerging countries. For example, in Brazil, Sony is an official partner of the 2014 World Cup. The objective is to improve brand awareness in a country where consumer electronics sales are expected to increase sharply. In India, Sony Pictures Television is already the provider of some of the top-rated television channels in the market. Hirai also wants to use the BRIC economies as a base to strengthen Sony's supply chain.[10]

HITACHI

History

Hitachi was founded in 1910 by Namihei Odaira, an electrical engineering graduate of Tokyo Imperial University. The company was initially a shop that repaired electrical equipment. The origin of the name

---

[10] BRIC: Brazil Russia India China.

is a combination of the two *kanjis*, *hi* (meaning sun) and tachi (meaning rise). It took inspiration from the Rising Sun Flag, the military flag of Japan. Hitachi's first product was a five-horsepower induction motor that was mainly used in copper mining. In 1924, the company manufactured Japan's first large-scale electric locomotive. In 1932, Hitachi started to produce elevators and completed its first electric refrigerator. In the 1940s, the company developed water turbines and power excavators. The Second World War slowed the activities of the group, but it recovered quickly and in 1958 the company was awarded the grand prize for its electron microscopes at the Brussels World Fair. A year later, Hitachi America was established. During the 1960s, Hitachi was Japan's industrial and technological backbone. The company developed an experimental nuclear reactor and constructed the first cars of the famous Japanese high-speed train: the *shinkansen*. It also launched consumer products such as air conditioners and washing machines. In 1971, the company developed the 1go storage unit and, soon after, built one of the most powerful nuclear power stations in Japan. At the end of the 1970s, Hitachi succeeded in trialing the world's first optical transmission system.

Due to its success, the company was listed on the New York Stock Exchange in 1982. Two years later, it started mass-producing the famous 256-kbit DRAM. In order to maintain its technological dominance, in 1989 the company opened four large R&D centers, two in the US and two in Europe. In the 1990s, it launched a subsidiary in China and established a new record with a computer that had the world's fastest processing speed. Another record was broken during the same decade with the *shinkansen*, which could reach speeds of up to 270 km/h. In 2002, it was the first company to develop a silent laptop with a cooling system, and in 2007, Hitachi developed EMIEW2, a small robot capable of interacting with its environment. In addition, in order to reduce Japan's dependence on rare metals, the company developed a method of recycling them. The company employs approximately 323,000 people around the world and its headquarters are located in the Chiyoda district of Tokyo.

Like many Japanese corporations Hitachi has always been eager to diversify into different business fields. Figure 2 shows the weight of each Hitachi business unit in 2012.

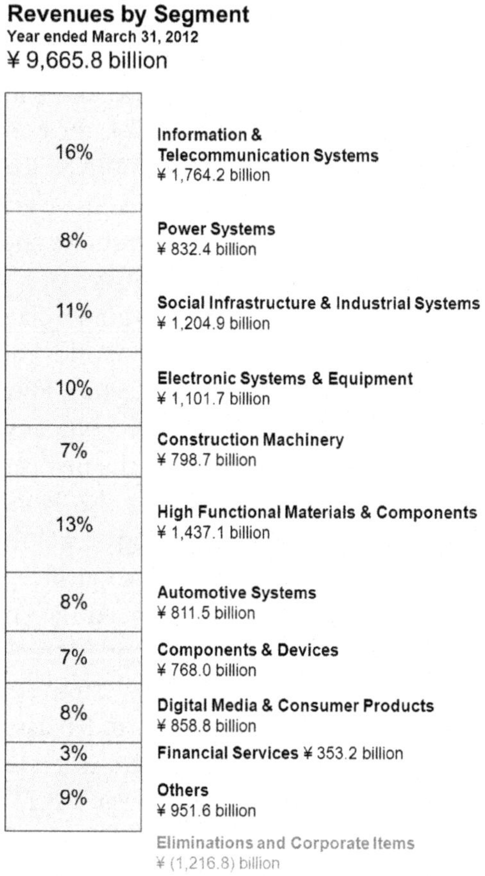

Revenues by Segment
Year ended March 31, 2012
¥ 9,665.8 billion

16%	**Information & Telecommunication Systems** ¥ 1,764.2 billion
8%	**Power Systems** ¥ 832.4 billion
11%	**Social Infrastructure & Industrial Systems** ¥ 1,204.9 billion
10%	**Electronic Systems & Equipment** ¥ 1,101.7 billion
7%	**Construction Machinery** ¥ 798.7 billion
13%	**High Functional Materials & Components** ¥ 1,437.1 billion
8%	**Automotive Systems** ¥ 811.5 billion
7%	**Components & Devices** ¥ 768.0 billion
8%	**Digital Media & Consumer Products** ¥ 858.8 billion
3%	**Financial Services** ¥ 353.2 billion
9%	**Others** ¥ 951.6 billion

Eliminations and Corporate Items
¥ (1,216.8) billion

Fig. 2   Hitachi's business units.

Note: I&T Systems: Software, servers, ATMs, system integration **Power Systems**: Nuclear/ Thermal/Hydroelectric power plant, wind power generation systems *Social I&I Systems*: Railway, escalators, elevators, industrial machines *Electronic S&E*: Semiconductors, medical electronics equipment, LCDs *Construction Machinery*: Hydraulic excavators, wheel loaders, mechanical cranes *High Functional M&C*: Wires, cables, magnetic components *AS:* Car information systems, engine management systems *C&D*: Batteries, information storage media *Digital M&C Products*: Refrigerators, washing machines, air conditioning *Financial Services:* Leasing, loan guarantees *Others*: Logistics, property management.

Hitachi in Recent Years

According to the Fortune Global 500, in 2012 Hitachi was the largest Japanese electronics company in terms of revenue. However, the corporation has recently seen turbulent years and has had to modify its business activities to get ahead in a competitive environment. The evolution of Hitachi's stock price shows that after a net decrease in the value of shares, beginning from 2008, the stock is now on an upward trend (see Appendix). The company saw four consecutive years of losses but returned to profit in 2011 despite a decrease in total revenue (see Appendix). The consequences of the 2007 financial crisis were serious for Hitachi, because there was a sharp decline in demand for most of the company's products.

At the beginning of 2010, Hitachi was experiencing the worst period of its 102-year legacy. In April 2010 Hiraoki Nakanishi became Hitachi's president and he implemented a restructuring of the company that resulted in two years of record profit. Nakanishi declared that to become a global player, the key factor is not revenue, but profitability. This statement serves as a guide to the group's transformation. Indeed, Nakanishi is trying to diminish the importance of consumer-related goods such as computer parts and flat-panel TVs to focus on global infrastructure projects such as power plants, rail lines, and water treatment facilities. Consumer business was forecast to account for less than 10% of Hitachi's revenue in 2012, half of its share the previous year. In parallel, its infrastructure business will account for 80% of its profit this year.

DEPARTING FROM JAPANESE MANAGEMENT TRADITIONS

One of Hitachi's main concerns was its hard disk business. Problems began to arise in 2002, when Hitachi bought IBM's HDD business to merge it with its own HDD division. However, the new unit did not make any profit. This is why in 2004 Nakanishi, a talented manager, was chosen to identify the main reasons why the group was losing money on this division. After two months, he declared that it was badly managed and that the only solution was to manage it himself.

He realized that there were problems with quality and said that 60% of the hard disk drives produced by Hitachi were not suitable for use. He hired experts from a competitor to reorganize the production and manufacturing lines. The business unit became profitable again in 2008.

But in 2010, on becoming president of Hitachi, Nakanishi decided that HDD should no longer be one of the company's core products, despite the fact that it was generating 10% profit margins. In March 2011, he sold the unit to Western Digital for $4.8 billion. By doing so, Nakanishi showed that all the business units of the group were included in the restructuring. He arranged the sale by arguing that the HDD industry was very fast moving and not well suited to a large conglomerate. Among the Japanese public this deal was not perceived well. According to traditional Japanese ideas, members of a company group (including units and their employees) should be supported for as long as possible. The idea of selling a profitable business was viewed very negatively in the Japanese press and left many observers stunned.

But Nakanishi then took even bolder steps. In order to reinforce its strength in the energy sector, Hitachi bought Horizon Nuclear Power (HNP), the British builder of nuclear power plants, in November 2012. Since the Fukushima disaster, the nuclear market in Japan has been idling. The takeover of HNP is intended to make it possible for the group to expand this activity abroad. Hitachi judges the international potential of nuclear energy to be promising, and Britain is one of the main markets in Europe. Hitachi plans to build two or three 1,300-megawatt plants in England by the mid-2020s.

On November 29, 2012, Hitachi created a partnership with Mitsubishi Heavy to combine their thermal power system businesses. Nakanishi said that this cooperation would help both firms to become global leaders in a tough business climate. Moreover, they want to become big enough to compete against overseas rivals such as Siemens and General Electric. Hitachi will take 35% of the newly created company. It will develop, manufacture, and sell turbines, boilers and other equipment for power and geothermal plants. The deal is supposed to be completed in 2014.

Nakanishi also wants to reduce the costs of the conglomerate. 20% of employees have been let go in under three years, and in April 2012 Hitachi delisted from the New York Stock Exchange because the low volume did not justify the cost.

Hitachi is also looking outside Japan to stimulate growth. Activities abroad now account for 57% of the revenue and 65% of the total employees. The company plans to develop procurement in other countries where prices are about 40% lower than Japan. A high priority for Hitachi is India. The group wants to triple its activity there before 2016. India needs infrastructure and Hitachi is strong in this respect. Hitachi also wants to use India as an export center for Africa and the Middle East, two other places where the demand for infrastructure is supposed to increase greatly in the near future.

CANON

History

Canon was founded in 1933 by a group of young people in a small apartment in Roppongi, a district of Tokyo. They wanted to produce high-quality cameras to compete against the German firms who were leading at that time. They quickly developed a camera prototype called "Kwanon" and a year later the Hansa Canon, Japan's first-ever 35mm focal-plane shutter camera, was born. The company continued its growth over the next few years by continuously developing technologies in the optical sector. In the 1950s, Takeshi Mitarai, the president of Canon, built a corporate culture which took as its key principle human respect and compassion, in dealings both with employees and customers. In 1955, Canon entered the American market, opening an office in New York. Two years later, the company set up its sole European distributor, Canon Europe, in Switzerland. At the end of the 1960s, exports already represented 50% of the total sales of the company. During the same decade, the Japanese firm was looking to diversify in order to reduce risks. In 1964, the company entered the office equipment market with the world's first 10-key electronic calculator. In 1967, the firm introduced a new slogan to illustrate its activities: "Cameras in the right hand, business machines in the left." Three years later, Canon developed the first Japanese plain-paper copying machine.

Up until 1970, Canon was achieving incredible growth. However, in 1974 the company struggled with financial problems due to the oil shocks and a defective calculator display component. The year after, for the first time in its history, the company did not pay any dividends. To compensate, Canon unveiled an ambitious project based on innovation that aimed to transform it into an "excellent global company." Under this plan, the company launched new products that had never been seen before, such as a laser printer with a semiconductor and a Bubble Jet inkjet printer. After its 51st anniversary in 1988, Canon started to promote environmental activities, such as toner cartridge recycling, in addition to globalizing its development sites. In the mid-1990s, Canon was still developing outstanding technologies but its debts became too large. Fujio Mitarai became the sixth president of Canon in 1995, and a year later he launched a new plan to optimize the financial structure of the company. The focus now was not on sales but on profit. In the 2000s, Canon maintained its world dominance in the digital camera market and has stayed profitable every year since. The company currently employs 200,000 people around the world, the vast majority of them in Asia. Figure 3 shows the weight of each Canon business unit in 2012.

Canon dominates the market in most of its activities and has strong brand awareness. According to Forbes, in 2012 Canon was the 35th most powerful brand in the world. It is ranked first among Japanese companies in the field of technology.[11] Canon is also a world leader in R&D; the company held the most patents in the US after IBM and Samsung in 2011.

Innovation Leader

As mentioned above, Canon is a global leader, making a profit every year. Due to its cutting-edge products, few competitors — besides its

---

[11] Only Toyota and Honda have a better ranking.

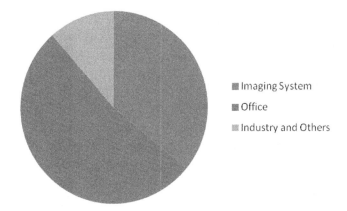

Fig. 3   Canon business units.

(*Source*: Canon annual report 2012)
Note: **IS:** Digital cinema cameras, digital camcorders, digital compact cameras and digital single lens reflex cameras.
Office: Office network multifunction devices, laser printers, solutions software, toner, photosensitive drums, toner cartridges.
I&Others: Semiconductor lithography, LCD.

compatriot Nikon — can seriously compete. These good results were achieved thanks to a management style based on a culture of excellence. Canon is active in just three different areas, and as such is more reactive to market change. The management of Canon wants to stay strongly focused on its core business. Since Canon only focuses on a small number of industries, the company has no choice but to strive to be number one in all of its endeavors.

In the past few years, Canon has faced decreased revenues due to the financial crisis but has stayed profitable (see Appendix). This contrasts with most of the other Japanese firms active in the electronics sector.

Despite such high aspirations, the group is conscious that it cannot rely solely on its own labs and that it will have to acquire foreign technology. That is why, in April 2012, Canon bought Océ, the Dutch printer maker. This take-over was an ambitious plan for Canon. The company paid $1 billion, its largest ever purchase. In acquiring Océ, Canon had two main goals. It wanted to strengthen its core activities and to diversify the risk of currency fluctuation. By keeping the manufacturing base in the Netherlands, Canon would spread the currency risk between the yen and the euro. With the same logic, in September 2012, Canon bought Iris, a Belgian company specializing in software solutions and information scanning.

Canon is also looking to optimize its supply chain by producing outside Japan. In June 2012, the company established a subsidiary in Brazil to manufacture compact digital cameras. Brazil is considered a lucrative place to invest, as it is forecast to grow rapidly due to hosting major sporting events, such as the FIFA World Cup and Olympic Games. Moreover, Brazil has the fourth-largest digital camera market after the US, China, and Japan. Increasing brand awareness in emerging countries is one of Canon's main concerns. In India, which is an important target for the Japanese firm, Canon rolled out a chain of branded retail stores called "Canon Image Square." The concept is very similar to the famous "Apple Store." Customers are able to handle Canon digital cameras and printers to experience them before deciding to purchase them. The group wants to increase the number of these stores in India from 50 at the end of 2011 to 300 in 2014.

Currently, everything seems to be going well for Canon; it is making a profit and is leading in many fields. However, the firm knows that being successful today does not necessarily mean being successful tomorrow. So the management is constantly trying to adjust its business activities to fit current trends. It is also preparing the company in anticipation of future troubles. Even if Canon is not directly threatened by any foreign conglomerates such as Samsung, another threat is already making Canon's strategy change.

Canon's Biggest Fear: Smartphones

The main advantage of smartphones is that they remove the need to carry other pocket devices. Unfortunately for Canon, one of the devices smartphones are beginning to replace is the digital camera. By proposing integrated cameras with an increasing number of megapixels, the next generation of smartphones may put fear into Canon's shareholders. The Japanese company has already reduced its forecast in revenue and profit for the coming years, mainly due to competition with smartphones. For Canon, being focused on fewer areas of business has been a strength until now, because it has been able to maintain and perpetuate its leadership. However, if one of these businesses is doomed, Canon may face huge difficulties in the near future.

Finding New Business Opportunities

However, Canon's management is sharp and has already started to anticipate how the group will adapt to this new threat. This is why the company has intensified efforts to enter into two new business domains: medical imaging and intelligent robots. In 2011, Mitarai, the president of Canon, said in an interview for the Japan Times that the company plans to expend 1 trillion yen in mergers and acquisitions within five years to improve its presence in these two sectors. He explained that he wanted to benefit from the strength of the yen to acquire companies abroad. For its medical division, the company wants to focus on diagnostic devices. The US — specifically Maryland, where one of the top "biotechnology clusters" is situated — will be where the R&D will be conducted. Canon has also launched a collaboration with the University of Maryland to develop an automated system providing infectious disease diagnostics. It will simplify the duties of the clinical staff and significantly improve the speed and efficiency of such activities. The goal of this partnership is to harness the strength of both institutions, to innovate, and to increase Canon's commercial portfolio.

With regards to intelligent robots, the main goal pursued by Canon is the automation of production. Japan is a world leader in robotics and Canon wants to be a major player in this sector. Instead of relocating all activities to countries where labor is cheap, Canon also wants to pursue the robot manufacturing of several products in Japan. The main goal is to cut costs. The company wants to move towards machine-only production in the next few years. However, the chairman has said that jobs will not be cut, and that workers will be transferred to do new kinds of work.

However, even if the fear of smartphones has pushed Canon to find new business opportunities for the future, the company still

believes that the digital camera market remains promising. The belief
is that by constantly innovating it can compete against smartphones.
During the Consumer Electronics Show in 2013, Canon presented a
new version of the digital camera: the PowerShot N.[12] The goal
pursued with the launch of this device is to create a new infatuation
for consumers who threaten to abandon digital cameras for smartphones. In addition to unique design and ergonomics, the device
provides the ability to take high-quality photographs, personalize
them, and then publish them directly to social networks *via* Wi-Fi
connectivity. The device also offers iOS and Android support. With
the PowerShot N, Canon hopes to reinvigorate the digital camera
market, where its popularity is slowly declining.

JAPANESE MANAGEMENT TAKING DIFFERENT ROUTES

As we have seen, Sony, Hitachi, and Canon have similar cultural backgrounds; they are traditional Japanese corporations and are confronted
with a world that is becoming increasingly competitive. Despite this
they have adopted different business strategies in order to grow.

In conclusion, these three cases reflect the seismic changes that
the electronics industry in Japan is undergoing. Panasonic, Sharp,
Toshiba and many others are also trying to change their core business
strategies because of similar problems. Thus, the general conclusions
that can be drawn for the three companies are also valid for much of
the sector overall. Being profitable in this new global environment is
the main concern of Japanese firms, a factor with which they were not
confronted during previous decades. The decline can thus be an
opportunity for them to entirely rethink their business model and
management style. If they succeed, these companies could emerge
stronger and regain their glorious pasts; if they fail, Japan could lose
its image as a world hub of high-tech electronics.

---

[12] See Appendix for more details.

QUESTIONS

1. What are the main reasons for the decline of the Japanese electronics industry?
2. Why do so many Japanese companies find it difficult to succeed in the globalized business world?
3. Which business strategy did each of the companies apply?
4. Are these strategies Japanese or Western?
5. Do you think they will be successful?
6. What management advice can you give to the three companies?

BIBLIOGRAPHY

Badenhausen, K. (2012). The world's most powerful brands. *Forbes*. (http://www.forbes.com/powerful-brands/) [8 January 2013]

Bembaron, E. (2013). Sony annonce son retour. *Le Figaro*, 8 January 2013.

Browning, J. (2012). Canon to combine $1 billion oce purchase after delay. *Bloomberg*. (www.bloomberg.com/news/2012–04–02/canon-to-combine-1-billion-oce-purchase-after-delay.html) [8 January 2013]

Fujita, T. (2012). Study finds the iPhone 5 is Japanese, in parts. *The Asahi Shimbun*. (http://ajw.asahi.com/article/economy/technology/AJ201210060045) [8 January 2013]

Hays, J. (2009). Japanese electronics industry. (http://factsanddetails.com/japan.php?itemid=922&catid=24&subcatid=157) [8 January 2013]

JCN Newswire — Japan Corporate News Network (2012). Sony and Panasonic to collaborate on the joint development of next generation OLED panels for TVs/Large-sized displays. (http://search.proquest.com/docview/1021954178?accountid=12156) [8 January 2013]

Jiji Press English News Service (2011). Sony to take full control of Sony Ericsson. (http://search.proquest.com/docview/900716446?accountid=12156)

Kageyama, Y. (2012). Canon eyes robot-only production for cameras. *Yahoo News*. (http://news.yahoo.com/canon-eyes-robot-only-production-cameras-101550562--finance.html) [8 January 2013]

La Tribune (2012). Hitachi et MHI s'unissent pour gagner en compétitivité dans les centrales thermiques. (http://www.latribune.fr/entreprises-finance/industrie/industrie-lourde/20121129trib000734086/

hitachi-et-mhi-s-unissent-pour-gagner-en-competitivite-dans-les-centrales-thermiques.html) [8 January 2013]

Mehrotra, K. (2012). Hitachi to triple India sales dwarfed by China business. *Bloomberg News*. (http://www.businessweek.com/news/2012-12-13/hitachi-to-triple-india-sales-dwarfed-by-china-business) [8 January 2013]

PR Newswire (2012). Sony computer entertainment to acquire Gaikai Inc., a leading interactive cloud gaming company. (http://search.proquest.com/docview/1022803615?accountid=12156) [8 January 2013]

Ramstad, E. (2011). Corporate news: Samsung to buy out stake in LCD venture with Sony. *Wall Street Journal*, 27 December 2011.

Riley, C. (2012). Fitch cuts Sony, Panasonic debt to junk. *CNN Money*. (http://money.cnn.com/2012/11/22/investing/fitch-sony-panasonic-downgrade/) [8 January 2013]

Saito, M. & Gloystein, H. (2012). Japan's Hitachi buys UK's Horizon nuclear project. *Reuters*. (http://www.reuters.com/article/2012/10/30/us-horizon-hitachi-idUSBRE89T0BB20121030) [8 January 2013]

Simms, J. (2009). South Korea's Rising Sun. *Wall Street Journal*, 5 November 2009.

The Japan Times, 12 January 2011. Canon plans Y1 trillion, give-year M&A blitz.

Wakabayashi, D. (2012). At Sony, Share Slide Underscores Test for CE. *Wall Street Journal*, 15 November 2012.

Wakabayashi, D. (2012). Hitachi president prods turnaround. *Wall Street Journal*, 11 May 2012.

Wakabayashi, D. & Inada, M. (2010). Questions grow on Japanese manufacturing quality. *Wall Street Journal*, 29 January 2010.

Canon official website. http://www.canon.com [8 January 2013]

Google finance. http://www.google.com/finance [8 January 2013]

Hitachi official website. http://www.hitachi.com [8 January 2013]

Morningstar. http://www.morningstar.com [8 January 2013]

Sony Mobile official website. http://www.sonymobile.com [8 January 2013]

Sony official website. http://www.sony.net [8 January 2013]

APPENDIX

Sony Stock

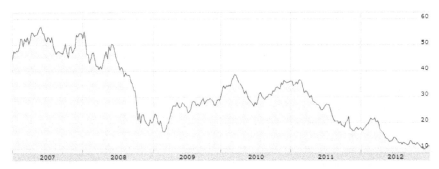

(*Source*: Google Finance)

Hitachi Stock

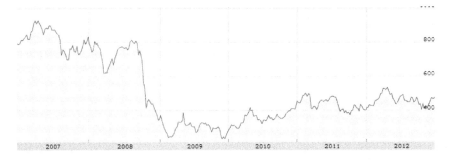

(*Source*: Google Finance)

Canon Stock

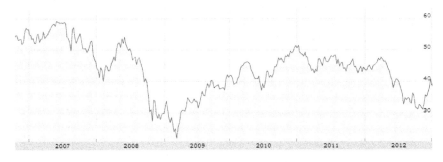

(*Source*: Google Finance)

Sony Results

(In JPY Million)	2008–03	2009–03	2010–03	2011–03	2012–03
Revenue	8,845,747	7,729,993	7,213,998	7,181,273	6,493,212
Net income	368,332	–98,938	–40,802	–259,585	–456,660

(*Source*: Morningstar)

Hitachi Results

(In JPY Million)	2007–03	2008–03	2009–03	2010–03	2011–03	2012–03
Revenue	10,248,483	11,194,237	10,000,369	8,968,546	9,315,807	9,387,587
Net income	–32,754	–57,932	–787,337	–106,961	238,869	103,958

(*Source*: Morningstar)

Canon Results

(In JPY Million)	2007–03	2008–03	2009–03	2010–03	2011–03	2012–03
Revenue	4,496,368	4,090,084	3,209,201	3,706,901	3,557,433	3,493,151
Net income	489,997	308,845	131,647	246,603	248,63	224,834

(*Source*: Morningstar)

Sony Xperia Z

Design:

 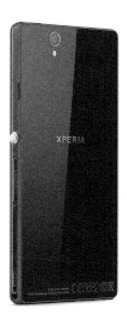

Characteristics

- 5" 1080 x 1920p full HD Reality Display with Mobile BRAVIA® Engine 2
- 13MP Fast Capture camera with Exmor RS for mobile, the world's first image sensor with HDR video for smartphones
- Dust and water resistant (IP55 & IP57) with a durable glass display
- 1.5 GHz asynchronous quad-core Snapdragon S4 processor with 2GB RAM
- Battery STAMINA mode improves your standby time by at least 4 times
- One-touch functions enable consumers to easily share music, photos and videos from their smartphone to an array of NFC-enabled Sony devices

- LTE, 4G for superfast entertainment
- A unique OmniBalance design with subtly rounded edges and smooth reflective surfaces on all sides

(*Source*: Sony Mobile)

Canon Powershot N

Design:

Features

- Built-in Wi-Fi® allows you to wirelessly transfer your images to social networking sites through CANON iMAGE GATEWAY#; to a PC or upload virtually anywhere on your iOS® or AndroidTM device* with the free download of the Canon CameraWindow app**.
- The convenient Mobile Device Connect Button allows you to connect to your AndroidTM or iOS® device* for quick and easy sharing.
- New Creative Shot mode uses composition, color and lighting from your original image to create five unique images with an artistic flair.
- Newly designed 2.8-inch capacitive, tilt, touch panel LCD; lens shutter; and zoom ring offer users a unique and creative way to capture photos.

- 8x Optical Zoom and 28mm Wide-Angle lens with Optical Image Stabilizer reduces camera shake so you achieve brilliant images.
- 12.1 Megapixel High-Sensitivity CMOS sensor combined with a DIGIC 5 Image Processor creates the Canon HS SYSTEM for improved low-light performance up to ISO 6400 and enhanced image quality.
- Capture stunning 1080p Full HD video with a dedicated movie button, plus zoom while shooting.
- Intelligent IS automatically chooses from six different modes to optimize image stabilization for the shooting condition.

(*Source*: Canon official website)

Section III

INDIA

Doing it the Toyota Way in India? Managing Unsettled Labor Relations at the Toyota Subsidiary in India

Christian Knuth

Toyota Kirloskar Motors Pvt. Ltd. has been operating as Indian subsidiary of Toyota Motors Corp. since 1999. There were tough times for Toyota Kirloskar's management during the early years at their production site. No less than four strikes and two factory lock-outs (one lasting for 53 days) led to serious confrontations between the management and the employees, represented by their labor union. Since the two largest cases of labor unrest were banned by the state government rather than successfully solved within the company, trusting cooperation between management and workers is not likely to develop in the short term. Toyota continues to expand in India, but the shadow of labor unrest will fall across their future investments unless they can get a grip on the workforce the Toyota Way.

TOYOTA EXPANDING OVERSEAS

The Toyota Motor Corp. was founded in 1937 in Aichi Prefecture, located in the center of Japan. The company began to grow very quickly in the period after the Second World War, keeping pace with Japan's high-growth economy. Toyota is currently the largest car manufacturer in the world. From a production rate of about 100,000 vehicles annually after the war, production peaked at 8.534 million vehicles in 2007 and decreased to 6.371 million due to the recession in 2009. Toyota has more than 50 production sites worldwide with about 70,000 employees (plus approximately 316,000 in affiliated companies).[1] Toyota's capital was about 397 billion yen (about 3.97 billion USD) at the end of March 2008. Sales in FY 2008[2] were about 26,300 billion yen (about 263 billion USD) with a capital investment of 1,480 billion yen (about 14.8 billion USD), while the net income was over 1,717 billion yen, equal to 17.2 billion USD.[3,4]

Toyota started to build up their overseas production base around 1990, when the domestic production growth rate of 200,000 additional units per year stalled due to the developing economic crisis in Japan. The total level of production stayed at about five million vehicles, with overseas plants slowly substituting for inland production. The deflationary trend of the yen made a rising number of exports unlikely, and the preferred strategy was to meet demand near production sites — which also lowered costs of transportation and labor, particularly at Asian production sites.

In the period from 2001 to 2007, when Toyota was rapidly expanding overseas production to meet growing demand, global production increased by nearly 600,000 vehicles per year until the peak. They started in 2001 at a pace of 3.4 million vehicles produced in Japan and 1.8 million overseas. In 2007, overseas production (4.3 million vehicles) exceeded Japanese production (4.2 million vehicles) for the first time. In CY 2009[5] production outside Japan was about 3.6 million vehicles compared to 2.8 million in Japan (4.2 million/4.0 million in 2008). More than 80% of global sales are now overseas (see Fig. 1).[6]

---

[1] Toyota Motor Corp. (2009). *Toyota in the World 2009 Databook*. (http://www.toyota.co.jp/en/about_toyota/in_the_world/index.html) [13 December 2010].

[2] The Financial Year (FY) starts at Toyota on April 1, ending on March 31: thus FY 2008 is 2007–2008.

[3] Toyota Motor Corp. (2006–2010). *Annual Reports*. (http://www.toyota-global.com/investors/ir_library/annual/index.html) [31 January 2011].

[4] 1 yen equals 0.01 USD, as of the exchange rate on March 31, 2008. http://www.finanzen.net/.

[5] Calendar Year (CY) starting on January 1 and ending on December 31.

[6] Toyota Motor Corp. (2009). *op. cit.*

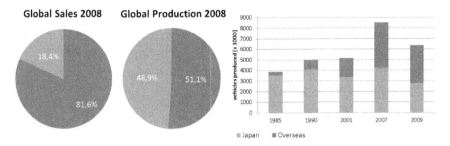

Fig. 1   Global sales (total 7.996 million units)/production (total 8211 million units) of toyota motor corporation and development of produced vehicles per year.[7]

These trends seem to continue. According to Toyota's vice president Takeshi Uchiyamada; "I feel Toyota is entering a new era in which the production base is being shifted overseas not only because the overseas production exceeded the domestic production but also because its growth rate is high. The basic idea of our global production is to produce cars where the demand exists".[8]

However, successfully raising the levels of overseas production requires securing Toyota's competitive advantage — namely, the Toyota Production System (TPS). Roughly speaking the TPS contains high quality and high efficiency processes combined with continuous improvement supported by the company's workforce. The transfer of the Toyota Way to India gives an idea of the challenge of implementing the TPS elsewhere, especially in an Asian low-cost labor environment. In the past, Toyota has combined high efficiency and high quality through its devoted workers — in large part, then, those devoted workers constitute Toyota's competitive advantage.

Moreover, the strategy of shifting production overseas means that the workforce must increase very rapidly to keep up the pace of production growth. From 2000 to 2006 the overseas workforce more

[7] Data taken from (Toyota Motor Corp. 2009), (Toyota Motor Corp. 2006–2010).
[8] S. M. Qumer and D. Purkayastha (2010). *Toyota Motor Company: Losing its Quality Edge?* ICMR Center for Management Research.

than doubled, increasing to about 120,000.[9] Transferring knowledge to the overseas workers from the mature production sites in Japan is thus a major issue. Toyota's future in India depends crucially on transplanting the Toyota Way and the company's philosophy across borders and between cultures.

PRODUCING THE TOYOTA WAY — OR, THE TOYOTA PRODUCTION SYSTEM (TPS)

In pushing forward the idea of expanding overseas production, Toyota will have to implement their globally-distributed production system worldwide, which means ensuring that Toyota's high efficiency–high quality production system is introduced effectively to production sites around the world. As mentioned above, this requires sustaining Toyota's competitive advantage.[10] Takeshi Uchiyamada described his vision, by saying:

"First, we must manufacture products of the same quality wherever we produce them. Second, the production base in each country has to secure international competitiveness. If we cannot do these two things, our global production does not work out ... If our overseas production grows at this pace, we have to figure out how to ensure the quality and quantity of our overseas human resources".[11]

The three pillars of the TPS are *Just-in-Time* (supported by the *kanban* system), *jidoka* (intelligent automation), and *kaizen* (constant improvement). *Just-in-Time* is supposed to maximize efficiency by procuring "just what is needed, only when needed and only in the quantity needed"[12] during the production process. The *kanban* system is an information system, which ensures that all processes are given

---

[9] T. Uchiyamada (2008). Toyota Entering Era of Global Production. http://techon. nikkeibp.co.jp/english/NEWS_EN/20080513/151583/
[10] S. M. Qumer and D. Purkayastha. (2010). *op.cit.*
[11] Uchiyamada, 2008. *op. cit.*
[12] K. Fumio (2006). Toyota and Asian Automobile Workers.In D.-o. Chang, *Labour in Globalising Asian Corporations — A portrait of struggle* (pp. 181–214). Asia Monitor Resource Centre.

relevant information about the following-on process. In addition, processes are highly standardized so that they can be performed quickly and safely. Standardization also allows easy synchronization of tasks, which is enhanced by defining different configurations. Operating with different levels of synchronized processes makes production flexible in changing to another efficient working procedure if necessary. Being able to change quickly and within a large number of production modes is important to adapting to fluctuating market demands.

Automation describes the practice of extensive use of intelligent machines in production, which calls for highly skilled workers to ensure that the machines are operating properly. Skilled workers take care of the different machines, and must be flexible in reacting to production line problems. *Genchi genbutsu* ("go and see") describes the process of checking what is the cause of a problem and correcting it right away. The workforce therefore has significant responsibility as well as a high workload.

Constant improvement, *kaizen,* can be understood as continuous monitoring and avoiding potential loss of efficiency in every process. Recognition of the potential for improvement, and working on production problems in, say, quality circles, calls for employees who truly care about these issues.[13]

Those pillars of TPS have enabled Toyota to improve their productivity, and are strongly linked with irregular working patterns and a considerable proportion of overtime work, which makes production highly flexible, as will be discussed later.[14] With regard to the impacts of the production system on employees, Toyota has a special need for good labor relations and is especially dependent on harmonious industrial relations between trade unions and employers. Whether this can be achieved in multiple cultural environments, or at least at Toyota Kirloskar in India, will be analyzed in the following sections.

"There is a sense of danger," said Koki Konishi, the general manager of the Toyota Institute, responsible for training Toyota's leaders worldwide. "We must prevent the Toyota Way from getting more and

---

[13] Fumio, 2006, *op. cit.*; Qumer & Purkayastha, 2010.

[14] Fumio, 2006, *op. cit.*

more diluted as Toyota grows overseas".[15] It was perhaps in India that this "sense of danger" became most acute.

TOYOTA KIRLOSKAR AND THE INDIAN AUTOMOTIVE MARKET

Toyota's Indian subsidiary firm, Toyota Kirloskar Motor Pvt. Ltd. (TKM), was founded in 1997 as a joint venture between Toyota and Kirloskar. The manufacturing plant is located in Bidadi, on the outskirts of Bangalore, in Karnataka State.

Toyota started its joint venture with Kirloskar by investing 7 billion INR (Indian Rupees) in October 1997. Initially they had a 76% stake while Kirloskar had 24%, though the ratio changed to 89% and 11% in 1999. Starting production in 1999, plant capacity was gradually increased from 20,000 units, to 35,000 units in 2000 and 50,000 in 2004.[16] The actual capacity of the Bidadi plant is about 80,000 units with approximately 3,300 people working there.[17]

Toyota first introduced the Toyota Qualis, in the jeep segment, to the Indian market in 2000, followed by the medium-class Camry and the small-car segment Corolla. In early 2005 they started producing the Innova for the premium segment, while taking the Qualis from the Indian market. Toyota's investment in Toyota Kirloskar had more than doubled by then, to 16 billion INR, equal to about 400 million USD.[18,19]

---

[15] M. Fackler. (2007, February 15). The 'Toyota Way' Is Translated for a New Generation of Foreign Managers. *The New York Times*. (http://www.nytimes.com/2007/02/15/business/worldbusiness/15toyota.html?pagewanted=1&ei=5) [15 January 2011].

[16] P. Mikkilineni and V. Gupta (2006). *IR Problems at Toyota Kirloskar Motor Private Limited*. Hyderabad, India: ICMR Center for Management Research.

[17] Toyota Kirloskar Press Release (2011, January 1). *Toyota in India*. (http://toyotabharat.com/inen/news/Sales_release2010.asp) [31 January 2011].

[18] Assuming an exchange rate of 40 INR equals 1 USD, as in April 2008 and since October 2011, according to http://www.bloomberg.com.

[19] S. Majumdar (2009). *Labour Unrest at Toyota: The Decision Dilemma*. IBS Research Center.

At present, Toyota plays a relatively minor role in the Indian automotive market compared to Maruti Suzuki and Tata Motors, but it aims to increase its market share to 10% from the current 3% by 2015.[20] The second production plant, which is in the pipeline, will boost Toyota Kirloskar's production capacity in India to 160,000 vehicles per year, about twice that of the past decade.[21] At the same time TKM's workforce has to grow considerably, increasing by about 2,000 workers, which requires closer attention to Human Resources Management issues (e.g. recruitment, industrial relations, etc.).

The automobile industry is a major driver of India's fast-growing economy. It accounts for more than 4% of India's GDP and is growing at four times the rate of the economy itself. Sales of passenger cars are expected to double to four million vehicles by 2015 and to hit nine million by 2020. However, there is a huge lack of investment, especially in the component industry. About 35 billion USD of investment is needed by 2020, while the automobile parts industry saw investments of only 1.7 billion USD in 2009–2010.[22]

Indian state governments are seeking to attract Foreign Direct Investment (FDI). There are many incentives for multinational firms to invest in India, such as low entry taxes, cheap water, and reliable electricity supplies, as well as special arrangements regarding pollution and safety issues, to name but a few.[23] Some state governments have amended labor laws in order to attract FDI (referring to restructuring, retrenchment, and closure of big firms), giving rise to

---

[20] Thaindian News (2010, May 13). *Toyota Eyes 10 Percent Market Share in India by 2015.* (http://www.thaindian.com/newsportal/business/toyota-eyes-10-percent-market-share-in-india-by-2015_100363174.html) [29 January 2011].

[21] Toyota Kirloskar Press Release. (2008). Toyota in India. (http://toyotabharat.com/index.asp) [31 January, 2011].

[22] Forbes India. (2010, December 6). *Restarting Trouble in Indian Auto Industry.* (http://www.moneycontrol.com/news/features/restarting-troubleindian-auto-industry_503398-) [30 January 2011].

[23] K. Shekhar Lal Das & S. George (2006). Labour Practices and Working Conditions in TNCS: The Case of Toyota Kirloskar in India. In D.-o. Chang, *Labour in Globalising Asian Corporations — A portrait of struggle* (pp. 273–302). Asia Monitor Resource Centre.

public concerns. Moreover, under the Industrial Dispute Act of 1947 it is possible for state governments to declare Special Economic Zones (SEZ) for specific industries in order to restrain trade union rights regarding strikes and collective bargaining. India is quite labor-intensive, with about 450,000 employees directly working in the automobile industry as of 2005 (and 10 million indirectly). Labor costs are relatively low, with average wages at about 200 USD, compared to 3,200 USD in the USA. In India labor amounts to only 15% of production costs, whereas the percentage is about 40% in Western countries.[24]

The production of automobiles grew hand-in-hand with the rise of domestic sales in India. From financial year (FY) 2004 to 2010 domestic sales more than doubled and seemed to recover quickly from the economic crisis. India depends on car imports, even though production has steadily increased over the last four years (see Fig. 2). Investment from Japanese firms was about 1,914 million USD between 1991 and 2005, making Japan the fourth largest investor over that period.[25] In 2004, Maruti Suzuki had the biggest market share at 45%, while Tata Motors and Hyundai were at about 16% and 13% respectively. Toyota Kirloskar's sales recovered in FY 2010, increasing by 36% after falling the year before by 15%, but current market share is still only about 3% (see Table 1).[26] However, TKM grew over 10% more strongly than the market in FY 2010. Now, TKM aims to triple their market share to 10% by 2015.[27] In order to achieve that ambitious goal, Toyota Motors is going to double production capacity, investing about 35 billion yen (about 350 million USD) in their second plant.[28]

---

[24] *Ibid.*

[25] *Ibid.*

[26] Thaindian News (2010, May 13), *op. cit.*

[27] *Ibid.*

[28] India PRwire. (2008, April 11). *Toyota to Build Second Plant in India.* (http://www.indiaprwire.com/pressrelease/auto/200804118705.htm) [29 January 2011].

■ Domestic Sales   ■ Domestic Production

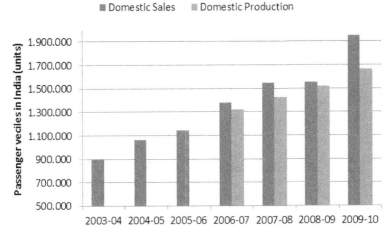

Fig. 2   Development of the Indian passenger car market.[29]

Table 1.   Toyota Kirloskar's position in the Indian automotive market.[30]

Fiscal Year	Sales of Passenger Vehicles in India		Production of Passenger Vehicles in India		Domestic Sales of TKM		TKM's Market Share
	Units	Growth	Units	Growth	Units	Growth	in %
2008	1.549.882	12,3%	1.426.000	7,8%	55.407		3,6%
2009	1.552.703	0,2%	1.517.000	6,4%	46.892	−15,4%	3,0%
2010	1.949.776	25,6%	1.662.000	9,6%	63.824	36,1%	3,3%

[29] Data taken from Ministry of Heavy Industries and Public Enterprises — India. (2004–2009). *Annual Report*. Ministry of Heavy Industries and Public Enterprises, Government India and Society of Indian Automobile Manufactures — SIAM. (2003–2009). *Industry Statistics*. (http://www.siamindia.com/scripts/industrysta-tistics.aspx) [31 January 2011].

[30] Author's calculation based on data from (Society of Indian Automobile Manufactures — SIAM, 2003–2009), (The Hindu Business Line (2010, September 20). Toyota Kirloskar Net Profit Zooms on Spurt in Sales. (http://www.thehindubusinessline.com/2010/09/20/stories/2010092050730200.htm)) [18 January 2011]), (Ministry of Heavy Industries and Public Enterprises — India, 2004–2009).

Sales growth of 36% in FY 2010 helped Toyota Kirloskar Motors to achieve a 47% increase in total income, which more than doubled the net profit compared to FY 2009. Total net profit after tax went up to 3,090 million INR, compared to 1,230 million INR in FY 2009[31] (from about 30.75 million USD to approximately 77.25 million USD). They also exceeded the net profit of FY 2008 (2,070 million INR), when sales had been better than in FY 2009.[32]

UNSETTLED LABOR RELATIONS

The story of difficult labor relations at Toyota Kirloskar starts about five years before the escalation of the labor dispute in 2006. Three other strikes had left Toyota Kirloskar struggling at the Bidadi plant. The first and second in 2001 started due to the management's announcement of a minimal wage increase on March 30th, which upset the workforce so much that they boycotted lunch on April 2nd. TKM's management ordered the workers to leave the factory and interrogated about 25 leaders inside the plant.[33] In the absence of a solution, workers started a sit-in the next day. Nearly two weeks later, management dismissed one worker for instigating others to strike. The investigation continued, aimed at the other leaders, who were interviewed on April 3rd.[34]

Facing the need to improve management–employee relations and the communication between them, the TKM management announced the formation of a Team Member Association (TMA) in April, intended to fulfill this role. This did not include any right of collective bargaining, but aimed to give employees a chance to express their needs to the management. Fifteen members were elected for the team, while one candidate, who had been an active leader during the first strike, was dismissed beforehand.[35]

---

[31] Assuming an exchange rate of 40 INR equals 1 USD, as on March 25, 2010, according to http://www.bloomberg.com/.

[32] The Hindu Business Line (2010, September 20). *op. cit.*

[33] Fumio, 2006. *Op.cit.*

[34] Mikkilineni and Gupta, 2006. *op. cit.*

[35] Fumio, 2006, *op. cit.*

The TMA members decided in June 2001 to register as an official trade union. Management felt offended by this move, which increased the employees' power, and one member, Mr. Renka Prasad, was dismissed for "non-performance." When the TMA asked the management to clarify why their committee colleague had been expelled, management refused to discuss the dismissal procedures and stated that the TMA's only concerns were the canteen and safety issues. TKM's employees went on a second strike that year for 12 days, demanding reinstatement of the three workers dismissed during the events. They also requested higher job security and a reduction of the length of training courses from three years to one year. The period was reduced by the management to two years, but no solution was announced for the dismissed workers.[36]

The third strike with which Toyota Kirloskar had to contend occurred in January 2002 and resulted in a lock-out by the management. The events lasted for 53 days and slowed down production dramatically. Beforehand, in December 2001, an employee had been dismissed although he had completed his training and performed well. After announcing the strike by Toyota Kirloskar Motors Employees Union in the beginning of 2002, General Secretary Mr. Shiv Kumar B. and Joint Secretary Mr. Raghu R. of the union were dismissed for bad performance. The workers started their 53 day strike,[37] requesting the reinstatement of their dismissed union heads and also protesting against the changed shift system. Since 2002 the company had wanted the workers to work in two shifts in order to meet increased sales. The first shift was from 8 a.m. to 4 p.m., the second from 8 p.m. to 4 a.m. Between the two shifts, workers were required to work overtime, sometimes for four hours. In this manner, Toyota Kirloskar aimed to achieve Toyota's high international standards, which in this case meant producing one unit every 4.5 minutes and operating with high flexibility through using Just-in-Time production to meet changing demands.[38] This step towards implementing

---

[36] Shekhar Lal Das & George, 2006; Fumio, 2006, *op. cit.*

[37] Fumio, 2006, *op. cit.*

[38] Mikkilineni & Gupta, 2006, *op. cit.*

TPS at the Bidadi plant increased demands on the employees, particularly regarding workload and stress.

In early March 2002 the strike was banned by the state government, which declared TKM's manufacturing essential (in effect, a SEZ), by reference to the Essential Services Act — forcing the workers to return to work.[39] In April, Toyota Kirloskar changed the shift patterns and, after negotiations, increased salaries by 2,500 INR, although dismissed workers were not taken back until an industrial tribunal in January 2006.[40]

THE DISPUTE ESCALATES

Labor disputes peaked after a fourth strike, causing a second lock-out at the Bidadi plant. This began on January 8th, 2006, and was declared by the Toyota Kirloskar management in response to the strike. After the conciliation process failed, the state government of Karnataka again prohibited the strike, once more declaring operations at the plant essential.[41]

The reasons for the escalation were rooted in events, which had happened about two years before. In September 2003, 27 members of an Executive Committee (EC) were elected, including seven committee leaders. In January 2004 the EC was preparing a charter of demands when two of their union colleagues were dismissed on the false grounds that they had threatened a supervisor. In reaction, employees protested by refusing to work overtime. Toyota Kirloskar's management suspended the presidential candidate, Ravi R., before the upcoming election. The union announced it would boycott the morning meeting, including the usual physical exercise before work.[42]

---

[39] Government India, 1981 — The Essential Services Maintenance Act: "3. Power to prohibit strikes in certain employments; (1) If the Central Government is satisfied that in the public interest it is necessary or expedient so to do, it may, by general or special Order, prohibit strikes in any essential service specified in the Order." (www.legalhelpindia.com) [11 January 2011].

[40] Fumio, 2006, *op. cit.*

[41] Shekhar Lal Das & George, 2006, *op. cit.*; Majumdar, 2009. *op. cit.*

[42] Fumio, 2006. *op. cit.*

After the morning meetings stopped, the management announced a wave of suspensions. In the first week alone, 12 union members were suspended, followed by another four over the next 20 days. Two of the sixteen were leading members of the EC, while another five were also members. The suspension letter gave no explanation, stating only "You committed serious misconduct".[43] Many of Toyota Kirloskar's employees felt very stressed and at risk of losing their jobs. Relations between management and workers were deeply distrustful. The Union Joint Secretary reported, "There are another 11 people suspended by the management and we fear they may also be dismissed. We are officially supposed to work for eight hours but we are overworked sometimes. And we are treated in such a way, that we can't even take a bathroom break when we want".[44]

In 2005 Toyota Kirloskar Motors Employees Union joined the Centre for Indian Trade Unions (CITU), and the company management started to acknowledge the union though not appreciating the connection to CITU. In April 2005 the management increased wages by 15%.[45]

The union's complaint about the dismissals at Karnataka High Court was rejected in October 2005, where it had aimed to obtain a declaration that the automobile industry was no longer seen as an essential service. In a next step the union asked the Division Bench, as a higher institution, to rule against the Karnataka High Court's judgment on November 5th. The process however, was not ended until the overwhelming events of 2006. In the meantime, 15 workers remained on suspension since April 15th, 2005. Serious trouble then began on January 5th, 2006, when Toyota Kirloskar dismissed three of the group that had been suspended. The management stated that intensive enquiries had proven all three workers to be guilty of bad performance and unruly behavior towards supervisors.[46]

---

[43] Shekhar Lal Das & George, 2006. *op. cit.*
[44] Mikkilineni & Gupta, 2006. *op. cit.*
[45] *Ibid.*
[46] Shekhar Lal Das & George, 2006; Mikkilineni & Gupta, 2006.

Following this statement, Toyota Kirloskar's employees went on strike the following day. Several reasons besides the arbitrary dismissal of workers can be cited for this. Heavy workloads and illnesses resulting from bad working conditions were serious complaints by many employees. Respiratory problems occurred because of a lack of safety equipment preventing paint and dust harming the workers.[47] The need to ask supervisors when one visited the toilet, as well as the enquiries regarding dismissed workers, were perceived as inappropriate and unfair.

Toyota Kirloskar's management argued, after establishing an indefinite lock-out on January 8th,[48] that the employees who joined the strike had planned to blow up the liquid petroleum gas tanks at the plant.[49] The management also declared the accusations brought by the employees' union regarding bad working conditions to be false, referring to their sophisticated health and safety guidelines and continuous auditing by the Safety Committee. In the face of the threats mentioned above and violence by the workforce, their only option was to lock the Bidadi plant completely. In addition, the strike was declared illegal, since Toyota Kirloskar Motors Employees Union had not given the requisite 14 days' notice before striking — a reference to the Industrial Disputes Act of 1947.[50]

With respect to Indian labor law, both the strike and the factory lock-out were illegal, as neither Toyota Kirloskar's workforce nor management had given prior notification.[51] Unfortunately, the ensuing conciliation process could not calm tempers. On January 9th,

---

[47] Fumio, 2006. *op. cit.*

[48] BBC News. (2006, January 9). *Strike Shuts Toyota Indian Plant.* (http://news.bbc.co.uk/2/hi/business/4594494.stm) [10 December 2010].

[49] Tribune News Service & PTI. (2006, January 18). *Strike Costs Toyota Nearly Rs 70 cr.* (http://www.tribuneindia.com/2006/20060118/biz.htm#4) [22 October 2010].

[50] Mikkilineni & Gupta, 2006. *op. cit.*

[51] ITUC CSI IGB (2007). *Annual Survey of Violations of Trade Union Rights — Toyota Fires Union Leaders, Locks Striking Workers.* (International Trade Union Confederation, www.ituc-csi.org/: http://survey07.ituc-csi.org/getcountry.php?IDCountry=IND&IDLang=EN) [31 January 2011].

Toyota Kirloskar's management and union members were requested to defend their stance before the Deputy Labor Commissioner in order to resolve the dispute. As management did not send anyone to the Commissioner's office, while several workers attended only in order to protest, the meeting was moved to January 12th.[52] The Commissioner suggested at the second meeting that the workers' terminations was not to be discussed until the Industrial Tribunal announced its judgment on the cases, and further that the lock-out be lifted and management abstain from any repressive measures considering striking employees. In order to resume production, all workers should stop striking and start working in an orderly manner. Finally, the state government of Karnataka resolved to ban the strike, since the Essential Service Maintenance Act for TKM was still in force, and passed the case on to the third additional labor court.[53]

The management subsequently announced on January 20th that it would end the lock-out on the following day if all the employees would sign a good conduct declaration when returning to the factory. Under the terms of the declaration, workers would agree to cease their indisciplined behavior, and would guarantee to perform in order that the company could once more operate at 100% plant utilization. The good conduct declaration also declared the strike illegal, and indicated that further events of this sort would cause disciplinary actions. The union stated that all workers are willing to end the strike, but would not agree to sign the declaration. Without the declaration however, management was not willing to let the workers return to work.[54]

Mr. A. R. Shankar, Toyota Kirloskar's General Manager for corporate planning, defended the declaration by arguing that "There is nothing in the declaration that constitutes unfair labor practice by the management. There are no changes in the service conditions either.

---

[52] Mikkileni Gupta, 2006. *op. cit.*

[53] The Hindu Business Line (2006, January 24). *Toyota Workers Call off Strike.* (http://www.moneycontrol.com/news/business/toyota-workers-call-off-strike_199264.html) [9 January 2011].

[54] *Ibid.*

The only reason for seeking such a declaration was the large-scale violence during the strike and the threat of the workmen to blow up LPG tanks in the company premises. Hence, we want to underline the basic fundamentals of employment through this simple document".[55]

On January 23rd the union said it would withdraw the strike, but still did not agree to sign the declaration provided by the management. One day later 1,000 workers returned to their workplace after the lock-out was lifted.[56] While management still declared that it was not willing to let workers in without signing because of fear for destruction, both parties started more promising negotiations on January 24th. During the talks, management accepted the union's demands for dropping the requirement for signing the declaration. These compromises ended the labor unrests at Toyota Kirloskar. Although the union initiated a short hunger strike on February 5th, this did not have negative effects on production.[57] Nevertheless, the trust between management and workers might have been seriously damaged by these incidents, and could be a serious burden for Toyota Kirloskar in the long run.

BACK TO BUSINESS

During the strike in 2006, economic impact was managed by keeping costs relatively low, but Toyota Kirloskar still lost about 700 million INR in total (about 17.5 million USD) due to production losses. Non-unionized workers were supposed to run the manufacturing process. About 700 emergency workers allowed the company to

---

[55] *Ibid.*

[56] The Hindu Business Line (2006, January 25). Over 1,000 Toyota Workers Return to Work. (www.the hindu businessline.com) [22 December 2010].

[57] The Hindu Business Line — 6. (2006, February 6) *Toyota Workers to Go on Hunger Strike.* (www.thehindubusinessline.com). [22 December 2010] and The Hindu Business Line (2006, February 11). *Trade Unions Form Body to Support Toyota Workers.* (www.thehindubusinessline.com). [22 December 2010].

maintain a vehicle production level of 30 units compared to usual 92 units.[58]

However, investment in the second plant was re-scheduled from 2007 to 2010, and Toyota's steps towards gaining further market share suffered from the delayed increase in production capacity. Even the backing of the state government of Karnataka could not lower uncertainty issues for Toyota.[59] It was reported by the Hindu Business Line that a strict labor policy and problems with bureaucracy were hindering Japanese investments, since only 0.2% of all Japanese FDI is aimed at India (China accounts for 9%).[60] Kiyomichi Ito, the chief of the other Toyota joint venture in India, Toyota Kirloskar Auto Parts, sees investment allocation from the following point of view: "Indians should understand that the capital investor has varied choices and China still remains an attractive destination".[61]

Analysts also stated that the confrontations between trade unions and management at Toyota, and in the case of Hyundai in 2005, had had negative effects on the Karnataka state government's attempt to attract Volkswagen to set up a plant in the region.[62] At the end of 2006, Toyota Kirloskar's management made a move to improve labor relations by announcing a revision of wages every year. In other Japanese companies in India, such as Maruti Suzuki and Honda, wages are revised only every five and three years respectively. Although increased wages are only relevant for regular workers, the 16% wage hike that year was seen as a positive sign. A management official said,

---

[58] Majumdar, 2009, Tribune News Service & PTI, 2006; Mikkilineni & Gupta, 2006. *op. cit.*

[59] BBC News, S. Raman. (2006, January 20). *Toyota India Plant Ends Lockout.* (http://news.bbc.co.uk/2/hi/south_asia/4631210.stm) [22 October 2010] and Majumdar, 2009. *op. cit.*

[60] The Hindu Business Line (2006, February 10). '*Labour Issue Delaying Decision on Toyota's Small Car Plant*' — *Japanese trade.* (www.thehindubusinessline.com) [22 December 2010] and Inter Press Service (2005, August 3). *INDIA: Japanese Investors Learn Indian Labour Laws the Hard Way.* (http://www.corpwatch.org/article.php?id=12531) [9 January 2011].

[61] Inter Press Service, 2005. *op. cit.*

[62] Majumdar, 2009. *op. cit.*

"We don't see wage increases as a burden but as an incentive for a work done well".[63]

In 2007, TKM founded the Toyota Technical Training Institute, which is supposed to educate young students specifically in four automobile engineering-related areas within a three-year full-time training course, including basic subjects like English, Math, and others. The desired outcome of this activity is to create highly skilled young workers who really care about Toyota. All fees and expenses such as housing, as well as some recreational activities, are covered by the training institute and practical training at Toyota Kirloskar is integrated within the studies.[64] On July 30th, 2010, the Training Institute announced the first ceremony for awarding 63 students their academic degrees on the successful completion of the three-year training course.[65] Toyota Kirloskar hosted 191 students between 2007 and 2010, and is hopefully thereby getting some new prospective workers to meet the need to boost their production capacity and attack market share in the Indian automobile sector.

In a joint interview with Hiroshi Nakagawa (managing director of TKM), senior managing director and Toyota board member Dato Akira Okabe discussed the relation between different approaches of implementing the Toyota Way, such as "evolve," "compromise," and "adapt" by proposing a mixture of these three:

"All of those had to be used. Yet, there is no fixed definition of the Toyota Way. People have a different image, a different understanding about it. Actually what it means is respect for human beings, the market and society ... We are now in a very important stage for Toyota in India. So the key is how to bring Toyota's experience to India and adapt it to Indian requirements.".[66]

[63] The Hindu Business Line (2006, December 5). *Toyota Kirloskar to Revise Wages every Year.* (http://www.thehindubusinessline.com/2006/12/05/stories/2006120503200200.htm) [22 December 2011].
[64] Toyota Motor Corp. — Sustainability Report. (2008). *A Year Since the Opening of Toyota Technical Training Institute* (TKM, India).
[65] Toyota Kirloskar Press Release. (2010, July 30). *Toyota in India.* (http://toyotabharat.com/inen/news/ttti_ceremony.asp) [31 January 2011].
[66] Businessworld. (2009, February 13). *Toyota Must Change.* (http://www.businessworld.in/index.php/Interviews/-Toyota-Interview.html) [10 December 2010].

Human Resources Management issues, referring to labor and industrial relations, might be relevant for Toyota's future in India. Recent quality issues at Toyota make the transfer of the Toyota Way even more important in maintaining the position of the world's leading car manufacturer. The question then arises of how Toyota Kirloskar is going to manage their labor relations in the long run, as Toyota announces the building of their second plant, 30 km from the Bidadi plant, with a total investment of about 350 million USD, almost doubling their current investments in India.[67]

Will Toyota finally succeed and get a grip on India in the Toyota Way?

QUESTIONS

1. How should Toyota Kirloskar manage their labor and industrial relations in the future?
2. Who are the important stakeholders and what are their interests?
3. How can the conflicts be explained by different attitudes towards management in India and Japan?
4. What role does international Human Resources Management play for a multinational company like Toyota Motors?

BIBLIOGRAPHY

Business Standard. (2006, January 12). Union Urges Action Against Toyota. Retrieved December 10, 2010, from www.business-standard.com: http://www.business-standard.com/india/news/union-urges-action-against-toyota/232751/

Dowling, P. J., Festing, M., & Engle, A. D. (2008). International Human Resource Management, 5th Edition. Cengage Learning EMEA.

Koen, C. K. (2005). Managing Resources: Human Resources Management. In C. K. Koen, Comparative International Management (pp. 198–253). Mcgraw-Hill Higher Education.

---

[67] Thaindian News (2010, August 29). *Toyota's Second Production Unit in India to be Ready by Dec.* (http://www.thaindian.com/newsportal/business/toyotas-second-plant-in-india-to-make-small-cars_10036934.html) [29 January 2011].

Nankervis, A., Compton, R., & Baird, M. (2008). Human Resource Management: Strategies & Processes, 6th Edition. Cengage Learning Australia Pty Ltd.

Rai, S. (2006, February 9). Labor Rigity in India Keeps Firms on Edge. *New York Times*, http://www.nytimes.com/2006/02/09/business/worldbusiness/09iht-toyota.html?_r=1. [22 October 2010]

Ray, K., & Roy, U. (2009). Toyota Motors in Emerging Markets. IBS Research Center.

Sivakamasundari, S. (2010). Toyota's Prius: Will it Emerge Successful in the Indian Market? Bangalore, India: Amity Research Centers Headquarters.

Toyota Kirloskar Press Release (2008, April 11). Toyota in India. Retrieved January 31, 2011, from http://toyotabharat.com/index.asp: http://toyotabharat.com/inen/news/corp_apr_08_sectkmplnt.asp

Section IV

KOREA

KIA Motors Facing Globalization Challenges

Marc David Hercaud

BRIEF HISTORY: FOUNDATION & RAPID GROWTH[1]

The South Korean automobile manufacturer KIA Motors was founded under the name Kyungsung Precision Industry on June 9, 1944. In the twilight of World War II, the company started its operations originally for the hand-manufacture of steel tubing and bicycle parts. From the very beginning, their headquarters have been located in Seoul, South Korea. In 1951 the company changed its name to KIA, deriving from the Sino-Korean word "ki" (to come out), and "a" (which stands for "Asia"): so the name of the brand could be translated as "the rising out of Asia".[2]

It is important to note that for a long time KIA operated as a so-called *chaebol* ("jay bol," meaning "business association").

---

[1] "KIA Motors Corporation — Company History." (http://www.fundinguniverse.com/company-histories/KIA-Motors-Corporation-Company-History.html). [26 January 2011]

[2] "Corporate Identity: Company: About KIA L KIA Motors." *KIA Motors Corporation.* (http://KIAmotors.com/about-KIA/company/corporate-identity.aspx). [1 February 2011]

Chaebol[3] can be seen as the Korean version of the Japanese *zaibatsu* which developed during the Meiji Era. They are originally family-held businesses that have strong ties with the State, which is their main source of capital — this latter feature marks their main difference from the *zaibatsu*, which to that end usually owned a bank. This type of State–corporate alliance was developed under president Park Chung Hee's regime (1961–1979) and permitted these conglomerates to achieve rapid economic growth through huge sources of funds. The state's incentive for this protection and financial assistance was that, despite the businesses being family-controlled, the *chaebols'* strategic decisions were mostly made by the government.

In 1962, the now-renamed KIA was producing motorcycles (production started in the late 1950s), when president Park selected it to concentrate on trucks and various industrial goods. Although being highly dependent on imports, KIA gained knowledge from its outside suppliers and gradually started to develop its own technology that allowed it to compete as an exporter of complete vehicles. Eventually, thanks to the construction of Korea's first fully integrated automotive plant in 1973, and in accord with the president's long-term economic plan ("Long-Term Plan for Motor Vehicle Industry Promotion"), KIA started to manufacture cars in 1974. Their first manufactures were the foreign brand car models Peugeot 604 and Fiat 132, followed by the first KIA model, named Brisa.[4]

Throughout the 1980s, still following former president Park's economic plan, Korea worked towards becoming an exporting rather than an importing nation, as it had been till then. Fearing that the domestic automobile industry was growing too quickly, the government set limits on the number of domestic vehicles that could be produced: KIA, along with Hyundai and Daewoo, became the only

---

[3] "CHAEBOL OF SOUTH KOREA." *San José State University.* (http://www.sjsu.edu/faculty/watkins/chaebol.htm). [26 January 2011]

[4] "Histoire De KIA | KIA Motors France." *Site Officiel de KIA Motors France.* Web. (http://www.KIA.fr/DecouvrirKIA/Histoire/Histoire_de_KIA/). [26 January 2011]

three companies allowed to manufacture cars. By the mid-1980s, KIA Motors was selling about 300,000 cars annually, making it the second largest South Korean automobile manufacturer. Enjoying limited competition in its core domestic market thanks to the rigid trade barriers imposed by its home country (in 1988, for instance, 305 foreign cars were sold in South Korea while more than half a million vehicles were exported), the *chaebol* was able to launch an aggressive and quite successful export campaign that aimed to penetrate the Japanese and European markets, among others.

A major turning point was when the company started shipping automobiles to the United States in 1987, the world's largest car market. This became possible thanks to an agreement signed between Ford and KIA, which made KIA the supplier of Ford's Festiva model. The company's strategy was clearly to replace Japan in the role of the leading supplier of low-cost cars, exploiting the crucial edge that Korea had in comparison to the developed markets: the cost of labor. Indeed, it was clear to the company's executives that Japan at that time was reducing its emphasis on cheap cars and instead was focusing on high-price and high-profit vehicles.

The early 1990s saw KIA suffer some major setbacks: the lifting of domestic trade barriers, powerful labor union strikes, which forced the company into a significant wage rise, and the renunciation of its *chaebol* structure in favor of independence. Regardless of these changes, the company continued its growth, and entered the mid-1990s as the 20th-largest automobile manufacturer in the world, exporting in some 80 countries including the flourishing Chinese one. Doing well at home, KIA was preparing to enter the US market with its own cars and dealers, requiring heavy investments in order to expand production capacity (from 650,000 cars in 1993 to 930,000 in 1994, requiring $3.3 billion in debt). The company set up KIA Motors America (a sales and marketing division of KIA Motors Corporation) in 1994 and KIA Motors Europe in 1995, while also building up the brand's first European plant in Germany.

But the Asian financial crisis, which struck in July 1997, devastated both the economy of South Korea and the business of KIA, resulting in the company's bankruptcy and a 51% acquisition by

KIA Motors Manufacturing Georgia in West Point

Source: "Why Kia Bet on Georgia." Mark Bernstein 30 Nov 2009 *The Detroit Bureau* (http://www.thedetroitbureau.com/2009/11/why-kia-bet-on-georgia/) [26 January 2011]

domestic rival Hyundai Motor Company in 1998.[5] The main reason for the bankruptcy was the huge debts the company had accumulated during its race to expand.

However, the company has managed to continue its international growth since then, symbolized by the opening of KIA Motors Manufacturing Georgia in West Point in February 2010,[6] representing an initial investment of $1 billion and capable of producing 300,000 cars annually. This was an occasion for KIA to celebrate its 15th consecutive year of increased US market share — a solid proof of its success.[7]

---

[5] "Koreans Place KIA Motors Under Bankruptcy Shield." *New York Times.* (http://www.nytimes.com/1997/07/16/business/koreans-place-KIA-motors-under-bankruptcy-shield.html). [26 January 2011]

[6] "List of KIA Design and Manufacturing Facilities." *Wikipedia.* (http://en.wikipedia.org/wiki/KIA_Design_and_Manufacturing_Facilities#KIA_Motors_Manufacturing_Georgia_.28KMMG.29). [26 January 2011]

[7] "KIA Corporate History." (http://www.KIAmedia.com/secure/milestones.pdf). [2 February 2011]

CURRENT COMPANY PROFILE

Nowadays, as Korea's oldest car manufacturer, KIA distributes its cars in 172 countries and employs 40,000 people, making it one of the biggest and the most well-known brands globally.[8] As of 2010 KIA's revenue is estimated at KRW 23.26 trillion — over USD 20 billion.[9]

As mentioned, the brand is part of the Hyundai-KIA Automotive Group, which now owns over 34% of the company.[10] With almost 5% the Korean National Pension Service is the second major shareholder of the company. Although both KIA and Hyundai are part of the same group, they focus on different targets groups. Indeed, as Hyundai mainly targets mature and wealthy consumers, KIA aims to reach a younger, more stylish and active market segment. In addition, differences exist in regard to the brands' marketing strategies. To take the most obvious example: KIA's brand logo, according to the company's website, is "designed to reflect the company's youthful and energetic image," showing the brand's will to "move forward in a lively and entertaining fashion".[11] Accordingly, KIA's brand slogan "The Power to Surprise™" stands for the commitment to surpass the customers' expectations through innovation and new exciting product attributes.

In addition to the early use of 360° communication (use of all the available contact points and lines of communication with the customer, including the Internet as well as inventing new ways of advertising), KIA began to use interesting and little-exploited channels such as mobile advertising and a cooperation with an Internet

---

[8] "KIA Annual Report 2009." (http://www.kmcir.com/eng/kire6000/kire6400. asp). [1 February 2011]
[9] *Ibid.*
[10] "Shareholders." (http://www.kmcir.com/eng/kire1000/kire1500.asp). [30 September 2010]
[11] "Corporate Identity: Company: About KIA L KIA Motors." *Kia Motors Corporation.* (http://www.kiamotors.com/about-kia/company/corporate-identity. aspx). [1 February 2011]

radio provider to create a brand music web radio.[12] For the US branch, KIA created an extravagant advertising spot and broadcasted it in college campus cinemas or during the MTV Movie Awards[13] in order to reach their core target. Alongside this, KIA also follows a strong sponsorship strategy, being an official sponsor of major sports events including the widely known FIFA Worldcup, the Australian Open and X Games Asia, as well as being a regular sponsor of WNBA, several soccer clubs (among others Atletico de Madrid, Spartak Moscow, Girondins de Bordeaux) and tennis players (Fernando Gonzalez, and Rafael Nadal as the brand's Global Ambassador).[14]

In 2007 the company introduced a new corporate grille design in order to provide its vehicles with another unique characteristic: the "Tiger Nose." Moreover, in order to deepen brand recognition even further, the corporate website of KIA has incorporated the Tiger Nose design as its banner.

THE AUTOMOTIVE INDUSTRY SITUATION IN FACTS AND FIGURES[15]

To understand the degree of success the company has achieved over the six past decades, and to understand KIA's context of operation more precisely, it is worthwhile glancing over some important facts and figures for the worldwide automobile industry.

---

[12] Peter Finocchiaro. "Kia Claims Mobile Advertising Outperforms Traditional Web Campaigns." *Mobile Marketer.* (http://www.mobilemarketer.com/cms/news/advertising/6746.html). [5 February 2011]

[13] "Kia Seoul Finds 'New Way to Roll'" *Online Marketing.* (http://www.brandweek.com/bw/content_display/news-and-features/direct/e3i0e4b3f51d8b5e233e-376ae41562f29ab). [5 February 2011]

[14] "Sponsorship: Experience Kia | KIA Motors." *Kia Motors Corporation.* (http://www.kiamotors.com/experience-kia/sponsorship/default.aspx). [2 February 2011]

[15] "Automotive Industry: South Korea." *Britannica Online Encyclopedia.* (http://www.britannica.com/EBchecked/topic/45050/automotive-industry/225684/South-Korea). [27 January 2011]

KIA Motors Corporation

Source: (http://www.kiamotors.com) [1 February 2011]

The Global Market

As of 2009, global production of cars and commercial vehicles is estimated at roughly 77,000,000,[16] with the number of cars and light trucks on the road in 2007 approaching 810 million.[17] According to predictions by the Detroit branch of the Boston Consulting Group, one-third of the world's future demand will come from Brazil, Russia, India, and China.[18] The Hyundai-KIA Group is currently just behind Ford as the world's fifth largest auto manufacturer in volume, with 4.65 million cars produced in 2009.[19] The top three in the industry are Toyota (Toyota,

---

[16] "OICA Production Statistics." *OICA.* (http://oica.net/category/production-statistics/). [1 February 2011]

[17] "Automobiles Trucks Market Research — Trends." *Plunkett Research.* (http://www.plunkettresearch.com/automobiles trucks market research/industry overview). [1 February 2011]

[18] P. A. Eisenstein. "Building BRICs: 4 Markets Could Soon Dominate the Auto World." *TheDetroitBureau.com.* 21 Jan, 2010. (http://www.thedetroitbureau.com/2010/01/building-brics-the-four-markets-that-could-soon-dominate-the-automotive-world/). [1 February 2011]

[19] "World motor vehicle production: World ranking of manufacturers year 2009." (http://oica.net/wp-content/uploads/ranking-2009.pdf). [1 February 2011]

1	China 13,790,994
2	Japan 7,934,516
3	United States 5,711,823
4	Germany 5,209,857
5	South Korea 3,512,916

Fig. 1   Car production statistics.

Lexus, Daihatsu; 7.230 million units), General Motors (Cadillac, Chevrolet, Opel, and others; 6.46 million units), and Volkswagen AG (Volkswagen, Audi, Bentley, and others; 6.07 million units). The top vehicle-producing countries in 2011 were China, the United States, Japan, Germany and South Korea.[20] (See Fig. 1)

In Europe, where KIA has been importing cars for almost 20 years, the range of the brand has gradually been expanded so that KIA faces a competitor in every sector except for luxury cars and the sports car market.

The South Korean Market

Since South Korea's automobile industry is not only one of the biggest global manufacturers but also the sixth largest exporter, it contributes significantly to the country's economy. There are three major brands operating in Korea: Hyundai Motor Company, KIA Motors Corporation, and Daewoo Motor Corporation (owned by General Motors, although the group is willing to sell the brand). They represent over 90% of the South Korean market, the rest is split between two other small manufacturers and imported vehicles.

Keeping Up Appearances?

It might seem, that everything is going well for KIA. The company is extremely strong on the domestic front, and has exported successfully

---

[20] "OICA Production Statistics." *OICA.* (http://oica.net/category/production-statistics/). [1 February 2011]

to almost everywhere on the globe. However, for KIA to be successful in Western countries turns out to be difficult.

Taking a closer look on the European market, where the brand has focused its efforts since 2005, several problems emerge. Like its *chaebol* sisters Samsung and LG, KIA is enjoying huge success in the Asian developing countries mainly because the prices of its products are significantly cheaper than those of its competitors. However, when it comes to the export of its vehicles to developed and mature markets like Europe, one of the company's problems appears to be dealing with the image of Asian — and especially Korean — companies abroad. Indeed, since KIA is able to produce relatively cheap cars thanks to the cheap workforce in Korea, the brand has a definite image in the consumer's mind. And this image could become a drawback compared with other automobile manufacturers, should it be associated with poor quality, a lack of reliability and safety.

This also seems to be one of the brand's major concerns. In early 2010, KIA implemented a new seven-years' warranty policy all over Europe,[21] which is five years longer than those from all the other automobile manufacturers on the continent. Simultaneously, the company ran a powerful advertising campaign for this new product feature. Moreover, KIA invested huge amounts of money into research and development in order to achieve five stars at the Euro NCAP crash test for one of its cars, the Cee'd, for the first time in 2007. [22,23] The combined effect of these two initiatives has helped the company to get a bigger share on the European market, but KIA sales remain minor compared with European competitors.

Brand Identity: The KIA Method

The other notable aspect on which the company is currently focusing is its identity and positioning with respect to its core target.

---

[21] "Garantie." *Site Officiel De KIA Motors France.* (http://www.kia.fr/garantie/). [2 February 2011]

[22] "YouTube — 2008 Kia Cee'd Crash Test." *YouTube.* (http://www.youtube.com/watch?v=iJtcI50JJ8A). [4 February 2011]

[23] "Kia Cee'd." *Euro NCAP.* 29 Aug, 2007. (http://www.euroncap.com/tests/kia_cee'd_2007/297.aspx). [3 February 2011]

Beginning in 2005, the company identified design as its "core future growth engine" on the European market, which led in 2006 to the hiring of Peter Schreyer as Chief Design Officer (CDO) for a complete restyling of KIA's lineup.[24]

Hiring an authority like Schreyer (Chief Designer for Audi from 1994 to 2002 then for Volkswagen from 2002 to 2005, winner of global awards, such as the red dot[25]) finally gave a face to the brand. This face was about to be turned into an identity:

> "In the past, the KIA cars were very neutral. When you saw one on the road, you didn't really know if it was Korean or Japanese ... I think it's very important that you are able to recognize a KIA at first sight".[26]

To make a change, in 2007 the new German CDO did indeed come up with a totally new feature, launched through the "Kee" and displayed at the Frankfurt Motor Show[27]: the "Tiger Nose".[28]

> "Tigers are powerful, yet kind of friendly. The nose is three-dimensional — like a face, not just a surface with a mouth drawn on it. From now on, we'll have it on all our cars" (Schreyer, 2009).[29]

---

[24] "Peter Schreyer." *Car Design News.* (http://www.cardesignnews.com/site/designers/whos_where/display/store4/item45209/). [1 February 2011]

[25] "Chief Design Officer: Design: Experience Kia." *Kia Motors Corporation.* (http://www.kiamotors.com/experience-kia/design/chief-designofficer.aspx). [1 February 2011]

[26] P. Maric. "We Interview Peter Schreyer Head of Design at Kia." *Car Advice.* (http://www.caradvice.com.au/60510/interview-with-head-of-design-at-kia-peter-schreyer/). [1 February 2011]

[27] "Interview with Peter Schreyer, Chief Design Officer." *Kia Europe — Press Website.* 2 Mar, 2010. (http://www.kia-press.com/presskits/motorshows/geneva 2010/interview with peter schreyer.aspx). [2 February 2011]

[28] P. Patton. "Ex-Copycats Find Their Own Styles." *New York Times.* 9 Apr, 2010. (http://www.nytimes.com/2010/04/11/automobiles/11KOREA.html?_r=1&ref=automobiles). [1 February 2011]

[29] A. Sloane. "Kia on the Straight and Narrow for Design of New Sedan." *NZ Herald.* (http://www.nzherald.co.nz/automotive-industry/news/article.cfm?c_id=500847&objectid=10568475). [2 February 2011]

KIA's Magical Tiger Nose

Source: S. Mehta, "Vellum Venom Vignette: Kia's Magical Tiger Nose." *The Truth About Cars.* N.p., 19 Mar. 2013. (http://www.thetruthaboutcars.com/2013/03/vellum-venom-vignette-kias-magical-tiger-nose/) [24 May 2013]

Schreyer indicated he wanted "a powerful visual signal, a seal, an identifier. The front of a car needs this recognition, this expression. A car needs a face and I think the new KIA face is strong and distinctive. Visibility is vital and that face should immediately allow you to identify a KIA even from a distance".[30]

Schreyer's idea gave the brand the spark that it needed. In the first quarter of 2009, when the KIA "Forte" launched, KIA's sales rose 6.7%, its domestic market share topping 31% compared to 24.6% the year before — just as Korean car sales overall plunged 15.2%. In the US their share gained 0.7% within a year, reaching 3.1% on May 21, 2009.[31]

Alongside this total redesign, KIA unleashed a new marketing drive, which included the kiamotors.com, advertising lines and sponsorship campaigns.

All these strong and quite well remunerated measures are definitely proof of the company's will to continue its growth around the world and especially in Europe. However, it is to be seen, whether

---

[30] Maric, "We Interview Peter Schreyer." *op.cit.*

[31] I. Moon, "Kia Motors' Cheap Chic." *BusinessWeek.* (http://www.businessweek.com/magazine/content/09_22/b4133058607966.htm). [2 February 2011]

these measures can help KIA to fully reach their goals or whether other decisions have to be taken.

CONCLUSION

The development of KIA over the past six decades provokes several questions regarding the very strong growth the company experienced in the early days, and the relative stagnation it now seems to be facing despite the vast changes that have occurred in the company's strategy and operations.

QUESTIONS

1. Please assess the company's situation in the global market.
2. Why is the current situation different for KIA on its domestic market compared with the rest of the world, and especially Western countries?
3. What would you have done if you had been in charge of the company's strategy from the very beginning and onwards?
4. What recommendations could you give to the head of the company to make KIA more successful at this moment?

Section V

THE PHILIPPINES

Brightening Philippine Airlines (PAL): Strategizing for the Future of Asia's Pioneer and Sunniest Air Transporter

John Paul D. Antes

THE AIRLINE INDUSTRY IN THE PHILIPPINES

Air transportation in the Philippines began as early as the 1930s, as a means of travel and freight delivery in a country comprising thousands of scattered islands. In 1931, the Philippine legislature granted one of the pioneering companies, the Philippine Aerial Taxi Company (PATCO), a 25-year charter to operate for both local and international flights. It provided short flights for the major islands of Luzon, Cebu, Leyte, and Mindanao. In 1941, PATCO was transformed to become Philippine Airlines.[1] In 1952, the Philippine government passed Republic Act No. 776, also known as the Civil Aeronautics Act, which created the Civil Aeronautics Board (CAB) and the Air Transportation Office (ATO). These are the offices vested with power to promote sufficient, cheap, and efficient passenger airline services and to fuel competition among air transport carriers. CAB is responsible for the economic regulation of the air transport industry; ATO, on the other hand, specializes on the technical aspect.[2]

---

[1] See http://www.jal.com/en/history/aircraft/50s/pick_51-60_01.html.
[2] W. Manula (2007). "Philippine Airline Analysis: The Evolution of Philippine Airline Industry." (http://www.airlines.nl\issue_36\36_Manula_Evolution_Philippine_Airline_Industry.pdf.) [3 December 2010]

In December 1973, during the period of martial law, a major shift in airline policy occurred when then President Ferdinand Edralin Marcos signed the Letter of Instructions Nos. 151 and 151A that repealed Section 4(e) of Civil Aeronautics Act. This established the one-airline policy for both international and domestic operations. PAL, being the country's flag carrier, in effect monopolized the country's air transport industry leaving the other two airlines, Filipinas Orient Airlines and Air Manila, to be shut down and absorbed.[3]

In 1995, the country's domestic airline industry was liberalized under Executive Order No. 219. The policy reduced regulations on tariffs and fares and on entry into and exit from the airline industry. As a result of liberalization the industry became more competitive.[4]

BRIEF HISTORICAL BACKGROUND OF PAL

Since its inception on February 26, 1941, PAL has been the leading air carrier in the Philippines. It operates both internationally and locally. It was founded by a group of businessmen led by Andres Soriano, who served as its first general manager, with former senator Ramon Fernandez as chairman and president. PAL's first flight — between Manila and Baguio — took place on March 15, 1941, with a single Beechcraft Model 18 NPC-54 as its first airplane. On July 22, 1941, PAL took over the Philippine Aerial Taxi Company and in September of the same year it was nationalized. PAL's smooth operations were interrupted by the onset of the Second World War and the Japanese occupation of the Philippines, which lasted from 1941 to 1945. The airlines became an instrument of military service, providing a means of transportation to evacuate American fighter pilots to Australia. However, the planes were destroyed during the war. On February 14, 1946, PAL resumed its operations after five years of war. On 26 July of the same year, PAL became the first Asian airline

---

[3] *Ibid.*

[4] W. Manula (2006). "The Impact of Airline Liberalizations on Face: The Case of the Philippines." (http://www.udp.edu.ph/~cba/phd/docs/manula_paper.pdf.) [3 December 2010]

to fly in the Pacific Ocean when its chartered Douglas DC-4 transported 40 American servicemen to Oakland, California with short stops in Guam, Wake Island, Johnston Atoll, and Honolulu. In December 1946, regular flights between Manila and San Francisco commenced. It was also during this period that the airline became the official Philippine flag carrier.[5]

In 1947, PAL's acquisition of more new Douglas DC-4s enabled the airline to commence services to Europe. In 1951 PAL leased its DC-3 — named Kinsei — to Japan Airlines,[6] later leading to Japan's founding of its own national airline. In 1954, PAL's operations were interrupted by the government's suspension of all long-haul international flights. It resumed services five years later. After three more years, PAL began servicing Hong Kong, Bangkok, and Taipei with Convair 340s, later replaced by Vickers Viscount 784s.[7]

GOVERNMENT ACQUISITION OF PAL

The Soriano family's control of PAL was threatened when Ferdinand Marcos rose to the presidency and became a dictator during the period of martial law. Marcos and his cronies controlled every major Philippine enterprise, including PAL. The airline was placed under the control of the Government Service Insurance System (GSIS), the mandate of which was to manage Philippine government employees' pension funds and loans. For almost two decades, PAL experienced consistent losses. According to Far Eastern Economic Review, during that period PAL was "hobbled by ineffective management and corruption," which were aggravated by PAL pilots and cabin crew defections to other airlines. More than 1,000 of PAL's licensed mechanics were lured to competing airlines in the 1980s,

---

[5] See http://www.fundinguniverse.com/company-histories/Philippine-Airlines-Inc-Company-History.html, [3 December 2010].

[6] See History of Aircraft 1951–1960, http://www.jal.com/en/history/aircraft/50s/pick_51-60_01.html. [3 December 2010]

[7] PAL History. (http://web.archive.org/web/20000605082153/www.philippineair.com/mn_abtpal.htm) [3 December 2010].

"exacerbating flight reliability problems," as the industry magazine Aviation Week & Space Technology put it.[8]

RE-PRIVATIZATION

After the 1986 Edsa People Power Revolution, a new PAL president was appointed — namely Dante G. Santos. He orchestrated a massive modernization of PAL's domestic fleet through acquisition of the Shorts SD360 in May 1987, the Fokker 50 in August 1988, and the Boeing 737-300 in August 1989. Few years after, the Philippine government decided to sell PAL to a private entity. On January 30, 1992, a 67% majority of PAL shares was transferred to PR Holdings, a private consortium led by Antonio O. Cojuangco, who was also elected as the new PAL chairman and chief executive officer on March 25, 1992. The issuance of a resolution of representation within PR Holdings resulted in the election of former agriculture secretary Carlos G. Dominguez as PAL chairman and president on March 1, 1993. Under Dominguez's leadership, two brand new Boeing 747-400s were purchased.[9]

THE 1997 ASIAN FINANCIAL CRISIS

In early 1997, PAL rebranded itself as "Asia's sunniest airline" and began servicing New York City using Newark Liberty International Airport via Vancouver. This resulted in the airline becoming financially unsteady, having made a huge acquisition of aircraft without clear profitable routes. In 1998 the Asian financial crisis struck the airline industry in the middle of PAL's re-fleeting program, aggravated by massive lay-offs and labor disputes. On September 23, 1998, PAL underwent a complete operations shutdown that lasted for two weeks. It was during that time that Cathay Pacific assumed PAL's domestic and international flights. On October 7, 1998, PAL resumed its operations — mostly domestic flights — after an agreement was reached

---

[8] See http://www.fundinguniverse.com/company-histories/Philippine-Airlines-Inc-Company-History.html, no date.
[9] See Tripatlas.com: Philippine Airlines.

between PAL management and employees. Three weeks later, PAL gradually restored its flights to California (Los Angeles and San Francisco) along with other international services. It resumed its flight operations in Asia, particularly to Tokyo, Hong Kong, Taipei, Osaka (*via* Cebu), Singapore, Fukuoka, Dhahran, and Seoul, as well as to Riyadh. On December 7, 1998, PAL submitted a 'stand-alone' rehabilitation plan to the Philippine Securities and Exchange Commission (SEC) due to the absence of a strategic partner. In 1999, PAL submitted revised business and financial restructuring plans to the SEC, which required US$200 million in new equity with 40% to 60% from financial investors, which can be translated to no less than a 90% transfer of PAL ownership.[10]

RECEIVERSHIP AND REHABILITATION

In its first year of rehabilitation in 2000, PAL earned approximately 44.2 million pesos, or more than 1 million dollars. This allowed the airline a break from six years of huge losses. PAL's ownership of its maintenance and engineering division was formally handed to German-led joint venture Lufthansa Technik Philippines (LTP) on September 1, 2000. PAL opened an e-mail booking facility in August of the same year. With net profit of 419 million pesos, equivalent to US$9.6 million, in its second year of rehabilitation (i.e., 2001), PAL made persistent gains and in 2001 alone the airline was able to restore flight operations in Bangkok, Taipei, Sydney, Busan, Jakarta, Vancouver, and Ho Chi Minh, while also opening new flight services to Shanghai and Melbourne, and a year later to Guam. In 2002, Mabuhay Miles was introduced, combining the airline's previous frequent flyer programs PALSmiles, Mabuhay Club, and the Flying Sportsman into one. In the same year, PAL RHUSH — or Rapid Handling of Urgent Shipments Cargo service — was re-launched. In 2003, an online arrival and departure facility along with a new booking system was introduced. By the end of that year, PAL acquired its fifth Boeing 747-400. In 2004, to mark the airline's 63rd year of service, PAL launched services to Las

---

[10] *Ibid.*

Vegas. This was also the year when PAL started services to Macau on codeshare with Air Macau, and restored its services to Paris and Amsterdam through agreements with Air France and KLM; however, the airline's flight operations to Paris were stopped due to a joint venture by Air France and KLM. PAL began services to Nagoya and restored flights to Beijing in March 2005. On December 6, 2005, PAL signed an agreement for the acquisition and lease of up to 18 Airbus A319-112s and A320-214s from Airbus and GE Capital Aviation Services (GECAS). The procurement was made in response to rival Cebu Pacific's increasing domestic market share due to the latter's massive re-fleeting program and aging Boeing 737 fleet.[11]

LEADERSHIP

In January 1995, the ownership and management of PAL was transferred to Lucio C. Tan who was and still is the majority shareholder of PR Holdings. With a US$4 billion modernization and re-fleeting program, the dream to transform PAL into one of Asia's best airlines within three years began in April 1996 when the carrier's fourth Boeing 747-400 was delivered. The acquisition of 36 state-of-the-art aircraft produced by Airbus and Boeing from 1996 to 1999 became central to the aforesaid program. These aircrafts include 8 Boeing 747-400, 4 Airbus A340-300, 2 Airbus A340-200, 8 Airbus A330-300, and 12 Airbus A320-200. Accordingly, the re-fleeting program made PAL the world's pioneer in using a full-range of new-generation Airbus aircraft.[12,13] PAL is governed by a board of directors supported by a board of advisors and officers. The board of directors are elected at the annual stockholders' meeting; the board of advisors are elected annually by the board of directors immedi-

[11] *Ibid.*

[12] Philippine Airlines, http://www.tripatlas.com/Philippine_Airlines [3 December 2010]

[13] Price Waterhouse LLP. (1994). Case Study on Privatization in the Philippines: Philippine Airlines, Inc. (PAL). Available at: pdf.usaid.gov/pdf_docs/PNABZ910.pdf [3 December 2010]

ately following the annual stockholders' meeting; the officers are either appointed or elected annually by the board of directors at its organizational meeting immediately following the annual stockholders' meeting.[14] To date, PAL has approximately 14,000 employees across the country.[15]

The present chairman, chief executive officer, and owner of Philippine Airlines is Mr. Lucio Tan, a Chinese Filipino business magnate who, according to 2010 Philippines' Forbes, is the second wealthiest businessman in the country with a net worth of US$2.1 billion. Aside from PAL, he also owns Air Philippines and another 300 companies including Asia Brewery, the second largest brewery in the Philippines, Tanduay Holdings, one of the world's largest rum makers, and Fortune Tobacco, the largest tobacco company in the Philippines (Forbes, 2010).

SLOGANS AND CORPORATE GOAL

PAL's current company slogan is "With us, You're Always Number 1," but prior to this PAL used other slogans like "Mabuhay" (literally: long live), "Asia's First Airline," "Welcome Aboard the Philippines," "Shining Through," "Pilipino, Para sa Pilipino" (Filipino, for the Filipino), "On the Wings of Change," "Asia's Sunniest," "With You All the Way," "It's About Experience," "Love at 30,000 Feet," and "Clearly No. 1".[16]

PAL's corporate goal is to re-establish its reputation as Asia's "sunniest" airline through expansion of its coverage to the United States, to increase international flight frequencies to Canada and China, introduce flights to other Asian countries as well as to New Zealand, and reinstate operations to India, Europe, and the Middle East, which were discontinued following the 1997 Asian Financial Crisis.[17]

---

[14] Philippine Airlines Directors and Officers (2010)http://www.philippineairlines.com/about_pal/directors_and_officers/directors_and_officers.jsp [3 December 2010]
[15] See http://www.fundinguniverse.com/company-histories/Philippine-Airlines-Inc-Company-History.html.
[16] See Tripatlas.com: Philippine Airlines *op. cit.*
[17] *Ibid.*

FACILITIES

PAL operates various aviation facilities in the country, including several training facilities for pilots and cabin crew such as the PAL Aviation School, the PAL Technical Center, and the PAL Learning Center. The aviation school provides flight training not only for its own staff but also for other airlines, government employees, and individual students. The PAL Aviation School facilities include 10 Cessna 172Rs, a Piper Seminole, and simulators for Boeing 737 and turboprop aircraft. Over 5,000 graduates from the aviation school joined the ranks of the pilots of PAL, other airlines, or the Philippine Air Force. The PAL Learning Center serves as the integrated center for Philippine Airlines flight deck crew, cabin crew, catering, technical, ticketing, and ground personnel.[18]

PAL has facilities for integrated airport ground handling services, cargo operations, and full catering services for its own and other airlines. These facilities comprise PAL Airport Services, Philippine Airlines Cargo, and the PAL Inflight Center. The company's airport services are responsible for ground handling for seven international airlines calling at Manila. PAL Cargo offers shipment services for airmail and airfreight throughout the country and abroad. The PAL Inflight Center houses fully equipped in-flight kitchens and a catering center that offers catering services not only for PAL but also for Japan Airlines, China Airlines, Korean Air, and Northwest Airlines.[19]

PAL also has a state-of-the-art flight simulator and data center. Its flight simulator is designed to simulate a Boeing 737, complete with sound and visual systems, and has the capability to replicate all flight conditions, including day, dusk and night operations. The PAL Data Center is considered one of the most comprehensive computer systems and radio communications networks in the country. It is the headquarters of PAL's information systems department, communications engineering, and other information technologies.[20]

---

[18] *Ibid.*
[19] *Ibid.*
[20] *Ibid.*

FLIGHT OPERATIONS AND ROUTE NETWORK

PAL hub-and-spoke route network is based from its two major hubs in Manila and Cebu, with the majority of its routes operating in Manila. From Manila and Cebu, PAL operates domestically to major cities and islands in the Philippines. Internationally, the majority of PAL's flights to other cities in the Asia-Pacific region, as well as to the United States, Canada, Australia, Japan, and Hong Kong, and other areas with huge populations of expatriate Filipinos, are operated from Manila and to some extent Cebu.[21]

PAL currently has four non-hub routes: Vancouver–Las Vegas, Singapore–Jakarta, Sydney–Melbourne, and Melbourne–Brisbane. In the past, PAL's international non-hub routes included Vancouver–New York and Zürich–Paris, as well as non-stop services to major cities in Europe. However, the events of the Asian financial crisis forced PAL's management to terminate these services. Middle East services continued beyond the period of crisis but eventually ceased to operate as consequence of escalating and fluctuating prices of fuel, oversupply of seats, and emerging Middle Eastern carriers. On March 2, 2006, PAL's management decided to discontinue servicing Riyadh, its last Middle Eastern destination, although it maintains code-share agreements with other carriers based in that region.[22]

Borrowing from the famous cliché "when one door closes, other windows of opportunities are opened," PAL expressed strong intentions to increase its flight frequencies to Canada and China, to commence flights in Cambodia, Nepal, Myanmar, and New Zealand, to expand its presence in the US by introducing services to Saipan, Seattle, and San Diego and restore operations to Chicago and New York. There are also plans to reinstate services to India, Europe, and the Middle East. However, the downgrade of the country's aviation status by the Federation Aviation Administration made it difficult for PAL to mount its operations in the United States. As an alternative, PAL turned to servicing Perth and Auckland. In March 2010, PAL

---

[21] *Ibid.*

[22] *Ibid.*

re-introduced services to Brisbane using Airbus A330-300 equipment, and improved its existing services to and from Sydney and Melbourne by upgrading Airbus A330-300s to Boeing 777-300ERs. It also reinstated its four-times weekly services to Riyadh with new Boeing 747–400 equipment.[23]

CHALLENGES

Financial instability, labor disputes, and tough competition, aggravated by the remnants of the Asian financial crisis, make it difficult for the Philippine flag carrier to spread its wings and soar high. This section provides concise information on what went wrong and why it is still proving difficult for PAL to regain its eminence as the "sunniest" airline in the region.

Financial Condition

PAL has experienced huge financial losses in the past few years. On March 31, 2006, PAL's consolidated total assets amounted to 100,984,477 Philippine pesos, an 11% decrease compared to 112,982,600 Philippine pesos balance as of March 31, 2005. By March 31, 2007, the company's consolidated assets had diminished further by 8%, standing at 92,837,849 Philippine pesos. The decline in PAL's assets was primarily due to a net decrease in property and equipment value, advance payments to aircraft and engine manufacturers, and declines in current and other noncurrent assets. As of March 31, 2007, other current and noncurrent assets fell by 29% to 2,960.4 million Philippine pesos and by 20% to 2,941.7 million Philippine pesos "due to the effect of re-measurement to fair value of certain financial assets and derivative instruments".[24] After carrying 17% more passengers in 2009 due to acquisition of additional aircraft and growth in the local market, PAL's annual income report showed a rise in revenues amounting to US$1.634 billion from US$1.504 billion in 2008. In spite of

---

[23] *Ibid.*

[24] PAL Holdings, Inc. and Subsidiaries Annual Report (2007),http://www.philippineairlines.com/Images/PHI-17Q-December%202007_tcm61-6305.pdf [15 January 2011]

this, PAL's expenses escalated as a result of more flight operations and higher maintenance costs aggravated by fuel price fluctuations: 44% of PAL's income operating expenditures is utilized for fuel consumption.[25]

Labor Relations Issue

PAL has a history of labor relations problems. On June 15, 1998, PAL retrenched 5,000 employees, including more than 1,400 flight attendants and stewards, allegedly to reduce costs and alleviate the financial downturn in the airline industry as a consequence of the Asian financial crisis. Represented by the Flight Attendants and Stewards Association of the Philippines (FASAP), the retrenched employees — particularly the 1,400 cabin crew — sought remedy through the judicial process and filed a complaint on the grounds of unfair labor practice and illegal retrenchment. It was a decade before it was finally settled, passing through the Labor Arbiter to the National Labor Relations Commission, then to the Court of Appeals, and finally to the Supreme Court. The Philippine Highest Tribunal favored the aggrieved party, and on July 22, 2008, in its 32-page decision, ordered PAL to "reinstate the cabin crew personnel who were covered by the retrenchment and demotion scheme of June 15, 1998 made effective on July 15, 1998, without loss of seniority right and other privileges, and to pay them full backwages, inclusive of allowances and other monetary benefits computed from the time of their separation up to time of actual reinstatement, provided that with respect to those who have received their respective separation pay, the amount of payments shall be deducted from their back-wages." The Supreme Court further explained that there had been a failure on the part of PAL to substantiate its claims of actual and imminent substantial losses. Although the Asian financial fiasco severely affected the airline, PAL's defense of bankruptcy and reha-bilitation were untenable; hence the retrenchment policy was not justified (as cited in Fonbuena, 2009).

As far as PAL's labor management is concerned, employer–employee relations remain the primary dilemma up to the present day.

---

[25] See http://www.cebu-philippines.net/philippine-airlines-income.html.

In August 2010, 25 pilots and first officers of PAL quit their jobs to seek greener pastures abroad. A PAL pilot's salary range was US$2,000 to US$3,000 per month, compared to the US$8,000 to US$12,000 that foreign airlines offered (as cited in Amojelar and Ordonia, 2010). In addition, issues of collective bargaining agreements (CBA) and retirement age,[26] as well as threats of strikes, still have the potential to paralyze PAL's operations (Philippineairlines.com/news, no date).

Competition

For more than twenty years, PAL monopolized the air transport industry in the Philippines. This came to an end in 1995 with the passage of Executive Order No. 219 permitting the entry of new airlines into the industry. The liberalization and deregulation of the Philippine airline industry have brought competition in the domestic air transport industry, resulting in lower airfares, improvement in the quality of service, and greater efficiency in the industry in general. At present, three airlines compete over international and major domestic routes — PAL, Cebu Pacific, and Air Phil Express (formerly known as Air Philippines) — while two main airlines are serving minor and short-distance routes — Zest Airways (formerly Asian Spirit), South East Asian Airlines (SEAir), as well as other small airlines.[27] Zest Airways is eyeing a merger with SEAir.[28] Air Phil Express is an affili-

---

[26] Under the existing CBA in PAL, male and female flight attendants hired before November 1996 would be retired once they reached 60 and 55 years of age, respectively, and those hired after 1996 would be retired at 45 for both males and females. Those hired after November 2000, however, would be retired by 40 for both males and females.

[27] W. Manula (2007). "Philippine Airline Analysis: The Evolution of Philippine Airline Industry." (http://www.airlines.nl\issue_36\36_Manula_Evolution_Philippine_Airline_Industry.pdf.) [Date of Access]

[28] M.G.S. Ramos. (2008) "Yao to Keep Asian Spirit Brand in Merger with SEAIR," BusinessWorld [Online]. (http://www.gmanews.tv/story/92562/Yao-to-keep-Asian-Spirit-brand-in-merger-with-SEAIR) [3 February 2011].

ate of PAL so technically speaking the only head-to-head competition is between PAL and its greatest rival, Cebu Pacific.

EMERGENCE OF CEBU PACIFIC

Cebu Pacific is a subsidiary of conglomerate JG Summit Holdings Inc. and controlled by one of the richest Filipino-Chinese families in the Philippines — the Gokongwei family, which also owns large malls and department stores (Robinsons Malls), food and beverage companies (Universal Robina Corporation), real estate and property development (Robinsons Land Corporation and Universal Industrial Corporation), banks (Robinsons Bank), a telecommunications company (Digitel Sun Cellular), and a petrochemical corporation in the Philippines.[29]

Cebu Pacific flies 1,401 times weekly within the Philippine islands and 264 times weekly in Asia. The airline only began operations in 1996 but has now emerged as the Philippines' largest domestic airline, claiming a 50% local market share in 2009 and 51% in 2010. Philippine Civil Aeronautics Board data shows that from January to March 2010, Cebu Pacific had 2,448,990 domestic and international passengers — 110,000 more than PAL's 2,339,788 system-wide figures. Regionally, Cebu Pacific is regarded now as Asia's third's largest budget airline with 32 domestic routes and 14 international destinations, and the world's 22nd largest low-cost carrier, according to the May issue of Airline Business Magazine.[30] In global rankings, Cebu Pacific also now ranks 65th in world airlines against PAL's 72nd.[31] The airline aims to reach higher passenger traffic and is expected to stretch

---

[29] See http://www.jgsummit.com.ph/.

[30] "Cebu Pacific now Asia's 3rd largest low-cost Airline" (2009). (http://www.travel-dailynews.com/pages/show_page/30967-Cebu-Pacific-now-Asia%E@%80%99s-3rd-largest-low-cost-airline.) [3 December 2010]

[31] "Cebu Pacific overtakes PAL in global ranking" (2009). (http://www.abs-cbnnews.com/business/07/01/09/cebu-pacific-overtakes-pal-global-ranking) [3 December 2010]

its lead even further with the acquisition of 15 new Airbus A320s over the next three years and a growing list of domestic and international destinations, while maintaining its current cheaper airfares (as cited in "Cebu Pacific overtakes PAL in global ranking," ABS-CBN News, 2009).

THE FUTURE

Although the legacy of the financial crisis continues to hamper PAL in its competition with Cebu Pacific, it remains a significant brand within the Philippines with a very large and technically sophisticated fleet of aircraft, and its recent mild decline in profits is unlikely to signify any fundamental problem with the company. There may be some marginal exchange of market share between it and Cebu Pacific, but their status as the joint champions of Philippine air transport is unlikely to change. Notably, though, both PAL and Cebu Pacific "staunchly opposed" the Aquino administration's recent moves to implement an open-skies policy through Executive Order 29, which aims to boost tourism by decreasing restrictions on foreign carriers.[32,33] It may be that both companies counted on stable long-term futures while they remained relatively sheltered by national policy. How they will fare in the face of greater international competition remains to be seen.

QUESTIONS

1. What are PAL's strengths and what kind of strategy does the company follow?

---

[32] "Foreign groups back open-skies EO," *Business Inquirer* [online], 22 March 2011. http://business.inquirer.net/money/topstories/view/20110322-327023/Foreign-groups-back-open-skies-EO.

[33] Already in January 2006 the Philippine government passed Executive Order No. 500-A, setting requirements for foreign airline access to Diosdado Macapagal International Airport (DMIA) in Clark and to Subic Bay International Airport (SBIA). Prior to this law, only four foreign carriers were operating in Clark; subsequently, 68 foreign airlines were given rights to fly in Clark and Subic.

2. Would you follow a different strategy? Which one?
3. What measures should PAL take in regards to growing competition?
4. Where do you see PAL in the future?

BIBLIOGRAPHY

ABS-CBN News (2009), Cebu Pacific overtakes PAL in global ranking,http://www.abs-cbnnews.com/business/07/01/09/cebu-pacific-overtakes-pal-global-ranking [3 December 2010]

Amojelar, D. and C. Ordonia (2011), PAL To Take 25 Pilots Back No Sanctions, Vows DOTC Secretary,http://www.manilatimes.net/index.php/top-stories/22895-pal-to-take-25-pilots- [15 January 2011]

Birger, J. (2006). "Second-Mover Advantage," Fortune Magazine [Online]. Available at: http://money.cnn.com/magazines/fortune/fortune_archive/2006/03/20/8371782/index.htm. (Accessed: 3 February 2011).

Estabillo, R. (2007). "Philippine Airlines Embraces Competition." Available at: http://online.wsj.com/article/SB119136526585946956.html. (Accessed: 15 January 2011).

Fonbuena, C. (2009). "Retrenching workers? Don't repeat PAL's mistake." Available at: http://www.abs-cbnnews.com/nation/02/06/09/retrenching-workers-don%E2%80%99t-repeat-pal%E2%80%99s-mistake. [15 January 2011].

Forbes.com (2010). "The Philippines' 40 Richest: #2 Lucio Tan." Available at: http://www.forbes.com/lists/2010/86/philippines-10_Lucio-Tan_FQVX.html. [3 December 2010].

"History of Aircraft". Available at: http://www.jal.com/en/history/aircraft/50s/pick_51-60_01.html. [3 December 2010]. http://www.fundinguniverse.com/company-histories/Philippine-Airlines-Inc-Company-History.html. [3 December 2010].

Maney, K. (2001). "First Mover Advantage No Longer Advantage." USA Today [Online]. Available at: http://www.usatoday.com/tech/columnist/2001-07-18-maney.htm. [3 December 2010].

"PAL Reveals Salary, Benefits of Cabin Crew" (2010). Available at: http://www.philippineairlines.com/news/cabin_crew_salary_benefits.jsp. (Accessed: 3 December 2010).

"PAL urges FASAP to Accept Offer" (2010). Available at: http://www.philippineairlines.com/news/PAL_offer.jsp. [3 December 2010].

Philippine Airlines News (2010) PAL offers P80-M to settle CBA with Flight Crew, http://www.philippineairlines.com/news/cba_flight_crew.jsp[3 December 2010].

The Birth of the WATERCCOOP in Cagayan de Oro City

Anselmo B. Mercado

April 20, 2010 was a historic day in Cagayan de Oro City (Phillipines). It was the day the Water Consumers Cooperative (WATERCCOOP) was born — a "first step, a giant leap" for the cooperative movement in this part of the world. The organizational meeting was attended by 86 persons on their own personal capacities, many of whom also represented about 24 cooperatives and 10 NGOs in Cagayan de Oro's proper and nearby areas.

More than two years before, on December 12, 2007, the cooperative idea, as an alternative to the current Cagayan de Oro Water District (Water District) set-up, was first discussed by a group of leaders from civil society. When the motion was made to convert the Government-Owned-Controlled-Corporation (GOCCorp) of the Cagayan de Oro Water District into a Consumers-Owned-Controlled-Cooperative (COCCoop), a resounding overwhelming "yes" was heard from the assembly. The chairman proceeded to discuss the bylaws and the articles of cooperation. Among the salient provisions that were debated and approved by the assembly were as follows:

Water Consumers Cooperative (WATERCCOOP)

Objectives and purposes

Among others, these included to undertake production, generation, transmission and distribution of water for residential and commercial purposes; to manage water services based on the principles of accountability, transparency and participation; to empower the water consumers to have ownership, control of and access to the basic utility.

Capitalization

Membership fee of ₱50 ($1.2) per member;

Total subscribed capital (25% of authorized capital) of 312,000 shares = ₱31.25 million ($767,000)

Total paid-up capital (25% of subscribed capital) of 78,000 shares = ₱7.81 million ($191,800).

Area of operation

Misamis Oriental Province

Field of membership

To include regular and associate members within the area of operation and non-members (persons and institutions) who invest in preferred shares.

Governance and Management

To be composed of an interim Board of Directors (BOD) of fourteen, an audit committee of three and an election committee of three to be elected by the assembly of members.

One of the immediate tasks of the interim governance team of the WATERCCOOP was to prepare the requirements for registration with the Cooperative Development Authority, and to submit the registration at the soonest possible time. Upon approval of the registration, another general assembly of members would be convened within 90 days in order to elect the first set of officers (i.e., the Board of Directors and committees) of the registered WATERCCOOP.

WHAT IS A COOPERATIVE: ITS PURPOSES; ITS ADVANTAGES?

A Cooperative and Its Purposes

A Cooperative, first of all, is owned and democratically controlled by its members (in the WATERCCOOP, by the member-consumers of water). This ownership and control give social empowerment to the consumer-members. Secondly, a cooperative democratically operates and manages a business enterprise (e.g., a water utility) that can economically benefit members. Thirdly, although a business organization, a cooperative is a "non-profit" organization. Finally, a cooperative is a model to redistribute wealth and resources for the common good. As a socio-business organization, cooperative members have shared rights and responsibilities, duties and obligations, benefits and risks. In this sense, the WATERCCOOP's main purpose is to empower the consumers economically and socially.

Benefits

As mentioned above, a cooperative is a "non-profit" business organization. The profits earned by the cooperative from its business operations are used to pay for operations costs; to pay-off liabilities (loans) that the cooperative may entail and finally to to set-aside some funds (e.g., reserve fund against losses, education fund, and other funds) for its stability and security.

One advantage of a registered cooperative is its tax-exemption privileges. After all the costs are covered, the "net surplus" or (net earnings) are distributed back to the members following a cooperative principle and system:

1. Member-investors earn dividends on his/her capital shares or investments;
2. Member-consumers get patronage refunds based on his/her water consumption payments; the coop may also directly lower monthly payment rates for water consumption (besides the patronage refunds) should the business performance show that it can afford to do it.

As a democratically owned and controlled business organization, the members possess two very important social powers that they may exercise in the membership general assembly: They gained the responsibility, right and power to hear and be heard on issues and matters affecting them as individuals. Also, they can demand for their rights and invoke the principles of transparency and accountability regarding cooperative affairs and operations. Further, they can elect officers and/or representatives in the cooperative government and management.

Advantages to the Community

When the Water District would be converted into a cooperative, several effects became immediately felt: First, there is devolution of power from a GOCCorp to the COCCoop, in effect to the Barangays,[1] where the member-consumers reside. This is all the more significant, considering that the transfer of ownership and control is for the common good, benefiting all sectors, like the government, the people and their communities. Moreover, the primary motive of a cooperative is to serve the community (not for profit), in order to provide water services efficiently and effectively to the communities. Finally, the people and their communities will learn greatly from the experience of a cooperative undertaking: working together, mobilizing their resources in order to address key issues and concerns

---

[1] A Barangay is the smallest administrative unit in the Philippines.

faced by the communities is a very positive approach to the development of people and communities.

WATERCOOP — HOW DID IT ALL START AND WHY?

A Brief Historical Background of the Water District

The Water District was the first water district organized in the Philippines under Presidential Decree 198, which ruled that all water districts in the country be government-owned. The city council passed an ordinance in 1973, approved by mayor Reuben Canoy, to create the Water District. It was mandated to provide water and other related services to the residents of the city. Initially, it was recognized as a quasi-government corporation. In 1991, the Supreme Court ruled that water districts become Government-Owned-Controlled-Corporations to be governed by a Board of Directors on a six-year term, appointed by the city mayor (or governor of the province or mayor of the municipality) under which the water district operates.

From the start, the Water District has had no stockholders. Although the Water District is owned by the city government (which initially had put up an amount of ₱41.5 million ($1,020,000) as donated capital), the Water District has been operating by itself as if it totally owns the enterprise. Profits earned by Water District have been plowed back to its operations.

Public Scrutiny

Early 2007, two big problems besetting the Water District had surfaced. First, the Bureau of Internal Revenue had assessed the Water District of unpaid taxes for the period of 1997–2003 which totaled ₱34 million inclusive of penalties and surcharges. The Bureau made some actions that jeopardized the Water District operations (i.e., letter of demand in January 2004, garnishment of the Water District bank accounts in April 2007, which was lifted that same month after negotiations, and the issuance of a levy on Water District properties in November 2007).

Moreover, problems arose from a questionable contract between the Water District and a water company regarding a bulk water supply project. The Water District and the Rio Verde Water Company, Inc. had entered initially into a "model agreement", demanding the latter to supply water to the Water District (a minimum of 40,000 cubic meters (m^3) per day at ₱10.45/m^3 (25 cents). The model agreement was later converted into a legal contract (prepared by Rio Verde) and signed by both parties. However, the Water District management had later discovered and pointed out some "discrepancies" between the original model agreement and the revised legal contract. As a result the water consumers had to pay higher water bills by as much as ₱1.45/m^3 of water based on a parametric formula in favor of the Rio Verde Water Company.

How could that happen? Regarding the contract, disturbing details came to the surface. Upon authorization by the Board of Director, the contract was signed by Water District's general managers. Two years later, two members of the Board admitted the board's negligence to carefully examine the contract prior to signing due to "time pressure". Also, at the time of signing the contract (December 23, 2004), the Rio Verde was an unqualified bidder, violating the government's bidding process.[2] Additionally, there was a failure of Rio Verde to submit eligibility requirements for bidding (e.g., three-year audited financial statements).

Those problems prompted some leaders from civil society (the cooperative movement, NGOs, etc.) in Cagayan de Oro to discuss about "cooperative-izing" the Water District.

Formation of the Study Committee to Cooperative Water District

In December 2007, civil society leaders held a meeting to discuss the idea of converting the Water District from a Government-Owned-Controlled-Corporation into a Consumers-Owned-Controlled

---

[2]Awarding of contract was on Dec. 9, 2004; Approval of contract was on Dec. 20, 2004; Signing of contract was on Dec. 23, 2004; however, Rio Verde was registered with the Securities and Exchange Commission not until Dec. 21, 2004.

Cooperative. A Study Committee was formed (with subcommittees) to look into the financial, legal, organizational, social, and technical feasibility of this possible conversion.

On February 28, 2008, the committee presented its first report (mainly an analysis based on the audited financial statements of the Water District as of December 31, 2005, with comparative figures of 2004 by the Commission on Audit). On October 24, 2008, a follow-up report was presented (again an analysis based on the Commission on Audit audited financial statements of the Water District for the year 2006). The following presents some highlights of the reports.

ECONOMIC ASPECTS

Findings of the subcommittee that looked into the business, finance and economic aspects of the Water District operations revealed some positive and negative points.

a. *High profitability:*

The Water District was seen as a highly profitable public utility monopoly enterprise dealing in a basic commodity (water). In 2005, the gross revenue was ₱349 million ($8,585,497), with a net income of $15 million ($369,004). In 2006, the gross revenue increased to ₱490 million ($12,054,137), with a net income of ₱50 million ($1,230,014). This means that for every Pesus of water bill that consumers paid, the Water District earned 4.5 centavos in 2005, and 10.2 centavos in 2006. The yearly profitability rate of the Water District operations was 8.2% in 2004, 4.5% in 2005, and 10.2% in 2006. If Water District were a cooperative in 2006, it could have paid dividends for members' shares of 15%, and also would have been able to give patronage refunds of 7% per member for their water bills.

b. *Illegal disbursements:*

The Water District 2005 audit report noted some questionable disbursements. The amount of ₱130.89 million ($3,220,089) was disbursed "without legal basis" and/or in violation of government-authorized standards. The Water District 2006 audit report also revealed similar "illegal disbursements" totaling ₱105 million ($2,583,054). In other words, for every Pesus of water bill that consumers paid in 2005 and 2006, 37 and 22 centavos respectively were spent "without legal basis". The "illegal disbursements" included the legally allowed travel per diem per member of the Board of Directors which was ₱800 per day ($20). The actual amount collected by each Board was ₱4,500 ($110) per day. The limit of benefits per Board member was ₱20,000 ($490) per month or ₱240,000 ($5,900) per year. The actual average amount collected per board member was ₱718,000 ($17,700) in 2005; and ₱930,000 ($22,900) in 2006.

The benefits of each Board included a year-end incentive of ₱100,800 ($2,480), a service incentive of ₱84,000 ($2,060), an anniversary productivity of ₱33,600 ($880), grocery allowance of ₱30,000 ($740) and financial assistance of ₱20,000 ($490). The Water District gave ₱720 ($17) to a retiring Board who served only for five years.

c. *Mismanagement and inefficiency:*

The Commission found several incidents, revealing questionable and inefficient management by the Water District:

The system's loss was estimated at 60%. Procurement of materials without bidding amounted to ₱15 million ($369,000) in 2005, and ₱8 million ($196,802) in 2006. The cash inflow was lower than the cash outflow in 2005 by as much ₱7.4 million ($182,042). This negative cash flow was due to huge payments to suppliers and personnel and to interest on loans.

d. *Recent developments at the Water District:*

Internal conflicts developed between the Board and the First Labor Organization of the Water District personnel (FLOW). The latter produced documents showing anomalies and other wrong-doings committed by the Board. Since FLOW lost its trust and confidence on the current Board to manage the Water District it went public. From April 2010 on, it informed the people through media and other means about the anomalies (e.g., the questionable contract with Rio Verde).

e. *Has the WATERCCOOP the financial capability to operate the Water District?*

With a capital structure consisting of an initial capital of ₱44 million from the city government (1973), a loan about ₱1.02 billion (2006), and retained earnings of about ₱405.85 million (2005), the Study Committee's economic analysis has shown that, if the WATERCCOOP would operate the Water District, the profitability rate would go up from 4.5% to 42%. Also the cash flow would increase from negative 7.4% to positive 42%.

These should be achieved by cutting down operational costs (i.e., illegal perks, system's loss, etc.); installing more efficient collections of receivables; as well as installing a capital build-up scheme by the WATERCCOOP (see Appendix). The effects of these would be a gradual decrease of loans and interest payments, and a gradual internal increase of members' investment in the capital structure of WATERCCOOP-Water District.

Organizational-Social Aspects

The Study Committee has looked into the organizational and social feasibility aspects of making the Water District a genuine cooperative. The Water District has about 70,000 water-meter connections (with consumers) spread over most of the 84 Barangays of Cagayan de Oro City. To organize a cooperative of this magnitude is definitely a big challenge and a formidable task. The large membership necessitates breaking-up into geographic chapters (or sectors) for practical purposes and democratic manageability. The cooperative democratic control principle (One-Man-One-Vote) will apply at this chapter level to empower the individual members to directly participate and get involved in the affairs of the cooperative that may affect them. Each chapter will hold a regular annual general assembly at which they will hear reports from management and officers, discuss and decide on issues, and elect the cooperative officers. The democratic principle is supposed to prevail at all levels of decision-making (i.e., chapter-level general membership assemblies, Board of Directors and committee meetings).

Like any business and human organization, a cooperative organization is not foolproof. It can fail because of many factors such as mismanagement, corruption and dishonesty of officers or members, as well as inefficiencies and ineffectiveness (e.g., being unable to deliver quality products and services at reasonable costs). Problems can also arise from unsupportive and disloyal behavior (e.g., not paying financial obligations promptly, etc.) or from a misunderstanding of how a coop should work. These factors have caused many cooperatives to become defunct. Many other cooperatives are struggling to survive in the face of a highly competitive business environment.

However, Region X (Northern Mindanao), including Cagayan de Oro, is one of the most active cooperative movements in the Philippines. Several vibrant and active "millionaire" cooperatives are in this region. In fact they have become models and leaders of the cooperative movement in the entire country.

All these cooperatives have become very successful because of the adherence to the cooperative ideology and values (including transparency, accountability, good governance, concern and care for others, self-help-mutual-help, etc.); their continuous education and development of members, officers and staff; and selecting (electing) officers with leadership qualities that include character (i.e., trustworthiness, good community reputation), competence (e.g., professionalism) and commitment to serve the community. Sound management skills have helped to achieve this goal too.

These experiences of Region X and the know-how of cooperatives that are available at Cagayan de Oro are the very resources that the WATERCCOOP will be able to tap for its organizational and management needs.

CONCLUSION

Many activities and venues have been tried to drum-up support from all sectors which included a signature campaign with a signed manifesto, personal follow-up and presentations to the city mayor, the city council and the congressmen, public forums, media presentations (TV, radio, local newspapers), community and Barangay meetings (called "pulong-pulong") as well as presentations and other advocacy activities (parade, fun-run, etc.).

The efforts to make the Water District a Consumers-Owned-Controlled-Cooperative have been started, the WATERCCOOP has been organized. Its supporters continue to pursue its objective with new strategies to confront the challenges on all fronts (social, economic, organizational, legal, etc.). Time will show, whether these will prove to be successful.

QUESTIONS

1. Government-Owned-Controlled-Corporation or Consumer-Owned-Controlled Cooperative? Which one do you favor? Why? Are there alternatives?
2. What are the biggest problems on the way to WATERCCOOP? How can they be solved?
3. What will be the challenges after a transition into a WATERCCOOP? How can they be met?
4. How does corruption block and hinder business and community activities?

BIBLIOGRAPHY

Annual Audit Reports of 2005 and 2006 of the Cagayan de Oro City Water District.

Commission on Audit, Region X, Government of the Philippines.

CDA Region X Statistical Reports 2010.

Documents. From First Labor Organization of the Water District, Cagayan de Oro. 2010.

Documents (i.e., Reports, Minutes of Meetings. Letters, etc.) on Crusade to Make the Water District a Cooperative (2007–2010).

Mercado, Anselmo B. (2005) Readings of Cooperatives. SEARSOLIN, Xavier University, Cagayan de Oro , Philippines, July.

Montalvan, Antonio J. II. (2004) A Cagayan de Oro Ethno-History Reader: Prehistory to 1950. Legacy Sales & Printing Press, Cagayan de Oro City.

Morse, Lawrence B. (Year) A Case for Water Utilities as Cooperatives and the UK Experience. North Carolina A & T State University, Greensboro, NC, USA.

Presidential Decree 198. (1973) President Ferdinand E. Marcos, Philippines, May 25.

Republic Act 9520: The Philippine Cooperative Code of 2008. Philippines, February 17, 2008.

Socio-Economic Profile of Cagayan de Oro (2005–2006), City Planning and Development Office.

Valleser, Jay (2008) Water District, Goodness Gracious! How Could You? (Two-part Column), *Mindanao Gold Star*, October 2008.

APPENDIX

CAGAYAN DE ORO CITY

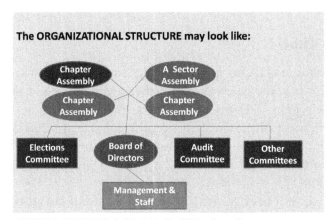

The ORGANIZATIONAL STRUCTURE may look like:

GENERAL ASSEMBLY: * GA elects the BODs, Committees
* One-Man-One-Vote Coop Principle at all levels

* BOD hires professional management & personnel

Brief History: Pre-Spanish, Spanish and American Era

During the pre-Spanish times, Cagayan was a small settlement on a hilltop called "Himologan" peopled by the local Higaunon tribe. In 1622, the first Spanish missionaries came and introduced Christianity to the local people, and they persuaded the people to relocate to the present location (where the St. Augustine Cathedral now stands) as a defense strategy against Muslim harassments. In 1871, Cagayan was made the capital town of the Province of Misamis and the seat of the Spanish government that included several nearby provinces. On December 26, 1898, the Spanish colonial government ended its 333 years of colonization. Freedom from Spanish rule was briefly enjoyed in Cagayan, only to be aborted by another colonial power — the American occupation of Cagayan from January 1900 to 1942. Then, the Japanese invaded the city and briefly ruled it, only to be taken back by the Americans in 1945. On July 4, 1946, the Philippines finally gained independence from America. Years of rehabilitation of the city followed after the devastating war. On June 15, 1950, Cagayan de Oro was granted the status of a chartered city. Historically, Cagayan de Oro indeed has always been an important town politically, commercially and culturally.

Current Times

Today, Cagayan de Oro is one of the fastest growing cities in the Philippines. It is the gateway to Northern Mindanao and the largest city in the region (56,966.84 has.), and the second highest ranking urban settlement in the great island of Mindanao. In 2007, the estimated total population of the City was recorded at 575,706 (total number of households was 116,574), with a growth rate of 3.12% (1990–2000).

Cagayan de Oro City is divided into two political districts. The first district comprises 24 Barangays and has a total population of 254,350 (51,347 HHs). The second district has 56 Barangays with a total population of 321,356 (65,227 HHs). The City is governed by the City Council, headed by the City Mayor, the Vice Mayor and 18 City Councilors (8 and 10 elected from districts 1 and 2 respectively). Each Barangay has its own elected Councils headed by the Barangay Captain.

The land use of Cagayan de Oro shows the following: 35.17% is agricultural, while 64.83% is non-agricultural comprising of 12.16% residential, 1.44% commercial, 0.22% industrial, 18.23% other uses and 32.78% open spaces.

In the aspect of education, Cagayan de Oro has been recognized as the educational center of Northern Mindanao. The City boasts of several high-standard private and government schools at the primary, elementary, high school (secondary) and college/university (tertiary) levels. The presence of these schools has been one of the attracting factors that have lured business enterprises and other people to locate in the city. In turn, this has given rise to various residential and housing ventures to meet a rising demand for decent housing for various economic levels of peoples.

The City's economy is diversified. Its agriculture production comes from food crops (rice, corn and vegetables), commercial crops (bananas, coffee, root crops, fruits and nuts), and from livestock (poultry, hogs, cattle, goats, sheep, horses). The City is also endowed with natural resources (metallic and non-metallic minerals, such as copper ore, limestone, sand and gravel). Its major industries (some 15,792 in 2007) include (a) wholesale and trade; (b) finance, insurance, real estate and business services; (c) community, social and personal services; (d) manufacturing; (e) construction; (f) transportation, storage and communications; (g) mining and quarrying; etc.

Section VI

CROSS-CULTURAL ENCOUNTERS

Visiting my Australian Friend's House

Mai Kaneshiro

I grew up in a small city called the Gold Coast, in Australia. At school, all of my friends were Australian, and I was basically the only Japanese in my year level. Nonetheless, I really got along well with them all, and felt no different to any of them, except for my race.

The cross-cultural incident that most sticks in my mind happened when I first went to an Australian friend's house for a sleepover. I was thirteen. Before I went to my friend's house, I had imagined that I would be welcomed by my friend's family in the same way that my mother treated my friends when they came over to my house. For example, if visitors come to our house for a night stay, my mother would treat the guests with the best hospitality — cleaning the room beforehand; preparing a great breakfast, lunch, and dinner; making the bed, etc. But this was not at all how I was treated at my Australian friend's house.

When I was welcomed to the house, the first thing I was told by my friend's mother was to "use the house as if it is your home." At first, I was really delighted by this, and I felt warmly accepted into the house. However, it was not until later that I really understood the meaning of her words.

As I entered, I noticed the difference from our house straight away. The room was dirty (it didn't seem as if any cleaning had been done before I came) and my friend's father was lying on the couch, wearing only shorts, and watching TV. In my house, there was no way my mother would allow any visitors to enter when it was dirty, and my father would definitely not be seen in such laid-back clothes when we had a guest. At that point, though, the disorganized room did not concern me much, because I just thought that her family must have been busy — however, I was embarrassed to see her father dressed like that.

But what surprised me most was the dinner my friend's mother prepared. Arranged on the table were bread, butter, pineapples (from a can), salami (not homemade), and instant soup. My friend, sitting beside me, was eating with delight; but the food left me honestly wordless. My mum would always make everything from scratch, and, if we had a visitor, she would make an especially extravagant dinner. The poorly made meal made me think, at first, that maybe my friend's parents didn't like me. But when I saw the rest of her family eating contently, I realized that this meal was normal for them. Even though I felt unsatisfied, I ate the whole meal to show respect for my friend's mother. But, still, I could not help but think how unhealthy and simple the meal was.

My friend and I cleaned up afterwards, and it was time for us to get ready for bed. But here again something concerned me: As I entered my friend's room I noticed that my bed hasn't been made. No mattress, blankets, nor pillow — nothing, basically, for me to sleep on. So I went courteously to my friend's mum and asked if there was anything I could sleep on, and she replied, "Of course there is! Why didn't you find it for yourself! Just open up those cupboards and I'm sure you can find everything you need!"

"Alright … ," I thought to myself, thinking that this was what she really meant by "use the house as if it is yours." My mum hated it if visitors opened any cupboard, drawers, or the wardrobe, so she always made sure they had everything they needed. So I was really surprised that my friend's mother left those things for me to do on my own, truly allowing me to do anything in the house. After that, I found everything I needed to sleep on, and made space in my friend's room so I could set up the bed.

The next morning, my friend and I woke up at 8:30. There was no breakfast ready: instead, we were told to make our own breakfast. On hearing that, I was yet again in shock, because when I had invited my friends to my house, my mum had prepared a deluxe breakfast, such as fruit salads, French toast, bacon, scrambled eggs, and many drinks to choose from. But obviously it wasn't like that here. So we ended up making scrambled eggs and toast together, which was rather simple but which I actually found quite enjoyable — my mother never allowed me to use the kitchen on my own because it is dangerous.

These were the things that I found most different from my culture when inviting people over. I remember that I was really surprised and astonished at the difference in the way Australian people treat their daughter's/son's friends when they come over. My first sleepover at my friend's place was honestly distressing and astonishing: I felt so "cheap," to be there and not to receive the hospitality I had expected. But as I grew older and came to be more familiar with the Australian culture, I noticed the way my perspectives changed. Now, I can definitely say that I would feel more comfortable going to a house where the parents left everything up to us, and for them to be their usual selves: this is because I would feel relieved to know that I'm not causing any annoyance. The reason I came to feel this way is by comparing it with my mother. Of course my mum shows better hospitality, and makes it seem like she is happy to have guests over; but I know that she gets tired from working so hard to make them feel welcomed. Also, my friends once told me that they feel like an outcast when they come over to my house, because they get treated differently: with too much care.

What I learnt from this cross-cultural experience is that it is really important to understand different cultures, and know how they think — because what you may be doing to make them feel better may actually be making them feel uncomfortable (just like my friends felt with my mum's hospitality). It may be better to recognize their cultural background before inviting them over: in this way, we can avoid disappointing people. For example, if a Japanese guest comes over, treat them in Japanese style; but if the guest is a Westerner it may be better to treat them like they are part of your family, and do nothing particularly special.

A Peck on the Cheek

Emi Inamoto

Have you ever had a moment when you were so surprised that each muscle contracts and refuses to listen to you? And you freeze like a deer that catches a glimpse of distant light in the middle of the highway at midnight? Well, I have. I was traumatized; I had never been in a situation like that; I didn't know what to do. And, looking at my reaction, she asked, "Are you okay? I was just being friendly. That's all."

It was in late September, and I was starting as a freshman in college. I had graduated from an international school in South Korea, and had never in my life experienced moving to a new school. So I was really excited — yet also nervous about meeting a new group of people with whom I would share my experiences with for the next four years. I was assigned to visit Chiba for an orientation camp. But who would have thought that my experiences at the camp would open a new segment in my understanding of the world?

As I got off the bus and dragged my petite suitcase up a hill towards the entrance, I gathered with students to engage in conversations. Nobody knew each other, and everybody was willing to talk; so I was introducing myself and where I was from to the other students. As I was doing so, I met an Italian girl who turned out to be the trigger of my experience. Even before I started saying my name, she walked towards me and hugged me hard and kissed me on both cheeks. I really was momentarily paralyzed. Then, her friend, who was from France, comes over and does the same thing; and then the

next, who was from South America; and then the next, who was from
Japan. I just stood there. I didn't know how to respond. I didn't
understand why a girl would kiss another girl, when they didn't even
know each other's names. Then a fifth girl tried to come up and kiss
me — and I took a step back, as if I was pushing her away. She looked
surprised.

In Korea, the only female that would kiss you is your mother; and
that is only when you are really young. No Korean, nor Japanese,
would ever kiss another person by way of greeting. As a matter of
fact, Asians in general do not do it. I was shocked.

After seconds of silence, she asked, "Are you okay?"

I was searching for words to answer that question — though the
question really only needed one word in reply. And, still out of control of my reactions, I accidently replied, "I do not kiss girls."

Now the girl was shocked, and the shock spread quickly to the
group of girls around her, which made the whole situation really
uncomfortable. But the Japanese girl quickly realized that I was not
used to this custom, and explained that it was their way of expressing
friendliness. Hugging and kissing on the face when you meet someone, she continued, is very normal and is repeated every time you
re-encounter the person or even when you say goodbye. She explained
that it expresses friendship, and doesn't have sexual connotations. So,
now that I think about it, it really was rude for me to say what I did.
She probably thought that I thought of her and her friends as taboo.

After hearing the explanation I felt really bad. I explained that
I had not been exposed to such a cultural practice, and I apologized
to the girls. After that experience, as I encountered more girls, I
adjusted and complied to the custom: the more greetings I gave, the
more natural it became. Now, I greet people with a hug and kiss as if
it is second nature — but I am also careful to whom I do it, because I
do not want someone else to think mistakenly that I am taboo.

Later in the evening, I was standing in line at the cafeteria to
receive dinner. The girls and I felt extremely close, as if we had known
each other for a long time. So, while I was waiting, as my natural
instinct, I put my arms around one of my friends' arms. I had no idea
it was making her feel uncomfortable; after we got our food, though,

she asked me why I had done it. I didn't understand her at first, and she became a bit upset and explained that she felt uncomfortable with me holding her arms the whole time.

In Korea, when you become friends, or get close to someone, you express your friendship by holding hands when you are walking or putting your arm around your friend's arm. However, in other countries, this is taboo. We were both confused about each others' behavior; I explained that it was normal in my country, and that it had no sexual connotations. She seemed a little skeptical about my answer, but the other Koreans who were at my table backed me up, explaining that girls do have bodily contact when they build up a friendship. After that incident, I take a lot of care when I am around my friends.

After the cultural experience at the orientation camp, I became careful about making sure my behavior was sensitive to other peoples' cultural backgrounds. I have learned that in other cultures, especially in Brazil, greeting a person with a hug or a kiss on the cheek is normal, even if you are meeting for the first time; but holding hands or having bodily contact with a friend is not, and is seen as taboo. However, in my culture, greeting is done at a distance when you first meet, and as you get closer you show your friendship by engaging in bodily contact.

From this experience, I learned that the best way to overcome such cultural misunderstandings is to communicate and try out different interpretations, before jumping to conclusions. In my case, talking about the problem and complying with others' behavior worked really well in helping me adjust to their culture. And it must be noted that, in an international environment where everybody has different cultural backgrounds, the greater the number of customs you understand, the more you will be guaranteed to avoid misunderstandings and conflict.

Index